DUTY
OR delight?

knowing where
you stand with God

tammie head

foreword by beth moore

LifeWay Press®
Nashville, Tennessee

Published by LifeWay Press®
© 2011 · Tammie Head
Second printing 2012

ISBN 978-1-4158-7126-3
Item 005429354

Dewey Decimal Classification 248.84
Subject Heading: SPIRITUAL LIFE \ GOD \ QUALITY OF LIFE

Printed in the United States of America

Leadership and Adult Publishing
LifeWay Church Resources
One LifeWay Plaza
Nashville, Tennessee 37234-0175

Going from Duty to Delight

CONTENTS

To my precious daughters, Peyton and Savannah—

Many are the prayers I've offered before God's throne on your behalf. All pale in comparison to this one:

For God to give you a heart that loves
Him beyond anyone or anything else.

All these years later His love still takes my breath away.

Please don't settle for anything less.

About the Author

Sitting on her bed in a tiny trailer, Tammie Head wondered what to do with her messed-up life. Growing up with every conceivable dysfunction, her heart started fraying as early as she can remember. Sin-filled exposure led to sin-filled living until fear, insecurity, and rebellious living became the only road she knew. In the darkest of hours, Tammie began to hear God calling her to Himself.

Rescued from the trash can of life, Tammie lives to tell of her wonderful Jesus who can redeem any life. Her utmost passion is for others to find the One who has captivated her own soul. Tammie Head loves opening the Scriptures with women of all ages. Women are drawn to Tammie's openness, honesty, passion, and grace. Most of all, they respond to her love for the Lord. Tammie is the founder of Totally Captivated Ministries. You can find more information on Tammie and her ministry at *tammiehead.com*

Tammie resides in Cypress, Texas, with her husband Erin and their two teenaged daughters Peyton and Savannah. When they are not busy with the affairs of life, all four Heads love to travel, enjoy loved ones, visit with friends, and serve together on the mission field.

Foreword

Dear One,

I am flooded with joy over the privilege of introducing you to my friend and fellow Bible study freak, Tammie Head. I first met Tammie when she was in her mid-twenties and had the strangest feeling even then that she'd make a mark on my life. I had no idea how much. Through the years God ordained our paths to cross often and with deepening meaning as we worshiped and served at the same fellowship of believers. Ultimately she became a spiritual daughter to me, and my love for her is the kind a heart possesses for blood family.

I am blessed beyond measure for the validation Scripture gives to these kinds of relationships. One of the greatest thrills of my life is watching God raise up younger generations of women to love His Son and to serve Him through studying and teaching Scripture. I get to cheer for many from a distance and praise God for His increasing fame through them, but I've gotten to watch a handful from close proximity. Tammie Head is one of them. And this is what I've seen:

> Tammie is a woman with a sustained passion for God. She is delight-fully new to many of you, but she is not new to the study of Scripture or to the teaching platform.

> Her daughters and her husband know the same Tammie that outsiders see. She is authentic and would be the first to want confrontation if she lapsed into performance.

> God is using the body of Christ to tell her to teach and speak. Her large weekly Bible class can't get enough of her, and word of her giftedness is traveling like wildfire.

Tammie's life leaves no other explanation except God. She has a back-story as rough as mine and some of yours. She reserves the right to keep parts of it private just as I do, but those of us who know her best can testify that she is a miracle of God.

She is disciplined in her personal pursuit of Christ. She genuinely loves Jesus and seeks Him as passionately and purely as anyone I know. She studies hard and pays the price.

At first glance, Tammie and I may seem similar in story and personality, but stick around and you'll see that she is her own woman in Christ and possesses her own unique gifting among His people. I think you are going to love her. I can hardly type these last words without clapping my hands. My dear sister, if you have never had the pleasure of meeting her before, with great joy I'd like to introduce you to God's servant, Tammie Head. Have a blast with her.

With love,

Introduction

Are you ready for some delight?

When did you last get so fed up over a situation that you finally put your foot down? I'm talking about a time when you were fuming inside with "Enough is enough!" Oddly enough, I'm hoping to take you to that spot in this Bible study.

I want to see your relationship with God become the thrill of your life. The flesh and the Devil have been kicking us all around far too long. Many of us have skewed views of God and don't even know it. We're spiritually frustrated, trying to keep all the rules and check all the boxes. Maybe we're even feeling a little dry, wondering where God went. We'd give anything to have a fresh encounter with the One who loves us so.

You really can know where you stand with God. Every single day. The way you've been wishing you could. Perhaps the way you've even seen others do. Overcoming the barriers and hindrances you feel with God is really yours for the taking.

We will explore six critical steps that will take us in our journey from duty to delight.

We will break down these steps into weekly sessions where we will gain confidence to rise up and take the place God has graciously given us. At times our content will plunge into the depths of spiritual introspection. You may find yourself wondering, *What does this have to do with duty or delight?* So I'll take the liberty to answer that question now. Everything. If you'll hang tight—giving yourself fully over to what you're learning—you'll see how giving God access to every inch of our lives directly affects our delight in Him.

The first three weeks deal primarily with God's pursuit of us. The second three weeks deal primarily with our pursuit of God in response to His pursuit of us. My hope in *Duty or Delight* is to help you answer the following questions:

How can I tell whether I consider God a duty or a delight?
How can I get to a place of delighting in God more?
Can finding God as a delight be a lasting work in my life?

We will predominately plant our feet in Ephesians 1:3-23. From these verses we will memorize specific truths to keep us confidently journeying the course of delight with God long after we close our Bible study. The truths we will behold have the power to change our lives from this day forward. How do I know this? I'm living proof.

How Our Journey Will Look

According to Scripture, discipleship involves four basic elements: connecting, growing, serving, and going.[1]

Not only do I see in Scripture the impact all four of these phases of growth have but I also see the impact all four have had in me. Connecting, growing, serving, and going have been vehicles God has used to transform my entire world.

In some ways I feel like Peter in Acts 3:6 when he stretched out his hand to the man and said, "I don't have silver or gold, but what I have, I give you: In the name of Jesus Christ the Nazarene, get up and walk!" If you will willingly take my hand over these next six weeks and walk with me in all four areas, I promise you will make progress in feeling more like that man: "Walking, leaping, and praising God" (v. 8).

I will challenge you to connect. Connect with God first and then with others. We will do this by gathering around God's Word and inviting Him to speak to us. I highly encourage you to do this Bible study within a small-group environment if at all possible. Connecting with other believers is vital to our personal growth as Christians, even if we're only gathering with one other person. Praying for one another and seeing God move in each other's lives are invaluable to our faith. God did not create us to live as islands. He created us for community.

I will challenge you to grow. So much of our Christianity can become about attaining biblical knowledge while never making it off the pages of Scripture and into our hearts and our steps. True discipleship means that we are living, breathing, and walking out God's Word in the dailyness of life—when we're at the office; when we're around extended family members; when we're happy, sad, perturbed, and all things in-between. God's Word changes how we live, think, act, and feel.

I will challenge you to serve. The more I read God's Word, the more I am challenged that serving others is what we are created to do. Most of our struggles for purpose can be explained with five words: We need to be serving. This Bible study addresses our God-given need by challenging us to think of ways we can serve those around us. I assure you that we will find a joy in Jesus by serving the broken, hurting, and needy around us. We cannot find that joy any other way.

I will challenge you to go. The message of the gospel is not meant to stay within the confines of our church walls. It's time we took Jesus to the streets! You will learn specific "Going" truths. These truths will be captured in what we will call Confidence Boosters based on a specific scriptural premise. I will challenge you to memorize them, marinate on them, and begin looking for opportunities to share them—perhaps with someone you know and maybe even with someone you don't.

We're going to pray each week and ask God to anoint us to speak these truths into someone's life. Then we will walk through the door in conversation when He opens it. Or we may even write someone an e-mail, text message, or a snail-mail note. Whatever we do, we'll be thinking in the context of actively "Going" with what we're learning.

I can hardly wait to do this Bible study with you. You are the reason I do what I do. Leading women to be totally captivated with Jesus grips me. And I've already offered a prayer for you to that end.

Hugs and love,

tammie

Be sure and check out the free support videos, suggestions for starting and leading a group, and service opportunity suggestions for your group at lifeway.com/tammiehead or at the Captivating Ministries Web site: tammiehead.com

1. LifeWay studies use the connect, grow, serve, and go labels to help you identify a balanced diet of studies and resources.

Going from Duty to Delight

FIRST STOP

Knowing God Has Chosen Us

Four common pitfalls keep us feeling unchosen. We may be falling for one, some, or all of them. Whether you struggle with one or all four, your delight in Jesus can grow. I hope you have your favorite shades handy. The blinding light of Jesus' love is gloriously stunning. This week we will look at four pitfalls that separate us from feeling the reality that God has chosen us.

Would you agree that life has a way of delivering serious blows to our confidence? Consider my friend who's in her early thirties. Beautiful and godly, she still continues to wait and wait and wait for a husband. She never would have imagined, say 10 years ago, that she would be walking the singleness road.

Sunday afternoon she sent me this text message:

Danielle texted … she got engaged this morning.

As happy as I was for her roommate, my heart sank for my friend. I could only imagine how she was feeling. We've been friends long enough for me to know how the enemy likes to play tricks on her mind:

Look at you.
You're not even desirable.
You will always be alone.
Accept it. It's your life.

I quickly dialed her number. Sometimes a text message doesn't do. Although my friend did not pick up the phone, I can assure you she would have heard me say, "Girlfriend, don't you dare listen to the Devil. You are very much so chosen."

If we were friends, how would you respond?

Have you had any blows to your confidence lately?

Are you letting God minister to you?

When did you last send or receive an e-mail or text that should have been a phone call?

Can I tell you something? I would say the same thing to you too. I'm going to say it—plus a whole lot more—through the pages of our study.

Dear Sister, what you hold in your hands has everything to do with my own journey. At one time spiritual performance gripped me so powerfully that God was more a duty than a delight. I didn't even know it. I just thought I had to keep God happy or else.

Spiritual performance can wear a person out. Not even the best of us can stay "on" all the time. The beautiful news is that God didn't save us so we would keep Him happy. He saved us for soul-satisfying intimacy.

I pray that you are about to be gripped by a great revelation over these next six weeks. It's not a new truth, just something we need to behold with fresh eyes and fresh ears. Here's the revelation: God deeply, deeply loves you. He loves who you are right now. The broken you. The one who wishes she was perfect. The one who beats herself up because she's imperfect. The woman who desperately wants to go up that mountain she's been circling for years. The one who can't seem to get her spiritual act together like all the "good Christians" she knows.

Do you know this girl? I bet you do. She's the one the God of all creation is crazy wild about and fiercely loves. She's you.

For some, this Bible study will be a time of recovery. Perhaps you've been in a tough place, and you need your sails reset. For others, it will be a time of refreshing. God plans on drenching you with a magnificent new vigor and vitality. Still others will experience a wonderful theological rebuilding, a much needed dismantling of things believed thus far, and a reassembling with new believing parts.

One thing is certain. You're going to learn how to put your foot down and stop putting up with what you've been putting up with. It's time for the condemnation to stop. It's time for the guilt to stop. It's time for the prayerlessness to stop. It's time for the fear to stop. It's time for all those false expectations to stop. **It's time you enjoyed your God.**

Which category do you think applies most to you? recovery? refreshing? dismantling and reassembling? Why?

_____

Imagine you presently, actively, fully delighting in God. What would that look like?

_____

Go back and look over the Suggested Service Opportunities at *lifeway.com/tammiehead* Have you considered how you might become the hands and feet of Christ in someone's life while doing this study? If so, what do you think you or your group will do?

Four Pitfalls to Feeling Chosen
1. **our twisted theology**
2. **our insecurity**
3. **our fear**
4. **our shame**

I Am Chosen

CONFIDENCE BOOSTER ONE

Scripture Premise:

"For He chose us in Him, before the foundation of the world, to be holy and blameless in His sight."

Ephesians 1:4

How do we begin combating these powerful obstacles? First we drench our minds consistently with the truth. To help us apply God's truth to our lives, each week we'll memorize a Confidence Booster along with the biblical basis for it.

The Confidence Booster and Scripture Premise will appear each week in the form you see in the margin. I encourage you to memorize these truths so that you can apply them to your life.

Pitfall 1

Our Twisted Theology

When I was a young believer, I heard a lot of preaching on pursuing God. All my church buddies and I were about being "on fire for God." We took our temperatures often by how ardently we pursued God. From the outside it looked really good.

Sadly, most of those believers I ran with back then hardly walk with God today. How can this be? Because most of us were living a faith based on how well we all performed for God.

How would you honestly answer?
○ **I've mostly envisioned God pursuing me.**
○ **I've mostly envisioned me pursuing God.**

I read something by A. W. Tozer that profoundly impacted my understanding. Think carefully with me about the following statement: **"Christian theology teaches the doctrine of prevenient grace, which, briefly stated, means that before a man can seek God, God must first have sought the man. ... We pursue God because, and only because, He has first put an urge within us that spurs us to the pursuit."**[1] Jesus' words from John 6:44 suggest this truth: "No one can come to me unless the Father who sent Me draws him."

Beloved, faith that begins with us is dangerous faith. When our faith originates with us, we're no better than Pharisees. We run the risk of religious self-absorption, never truly seeing God as He really is and missing out on the abundant life God gives.

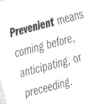
Prevenient means coming before, anticipating, or preceeding.

Listen to me: The very impulse you and I have to walk with God originates with God. Tozer adds, "It is by this prevenient drawing that God takes from us every vestige of credit for the act of coming. ... All the time we are pursuing Him we are already in His hand."[2]

How do you think your relationship
with God might change if you
believed this wholeheartedly?

> "I am sure of this,
> that He who started a
> good work in you will carry
> it on to completion until the
> day of Christ Jesus."
>
> **PHILIPPIANS 1:6**

What does Philippians 1:6 in the margin
suggest to you about God's pursuit of us?

A faith that originates with us paves the way for a lack of spiritual rest. Frustration, discouragement, weariness, and discontent can be by-products of a self-based faith. How? Because Christianity is all about Christ.

Christ stands always as the Alpha and Omega who began the good work of faith in us and wholly brings it to completion. Until we grasp this with our entire being (not head knowledge but heart knowledge), our faith will have the propensity to swing between spiritual defeat and spiritual conceit.

Have you found this true in your
own life? If so, how?

When I was a new Christian, I struggled with this immensely. For one, I thought I could lose my salvation. (You can't. Salvation "is not from your-selves" Eph. 2:8-9.) Being a person who already struggled with trying to be perfect all the time, this obviously led to a lot of fear and frustration.

When God saved me, I went from striving for earthly perfection to striving for spiritual perfection. I wore myself out keeping everything in check. Then when life came crashing down around me with situations I couldn't control, it wasn't so easy to get my game face on. Determination eluded me when a precious loved one was raped and I couldn't do a thing about it. Or when I was up all night with crying babies and desperately needed to shut my eyes for sheer sanity. Or when my marriage was just stitches away from unraveling.

All of these, whether great or small, rocked my sense of control. I had no idea my theology needed tweaking until God began to show me.

EP   How would you rate your tendency toward earthly perfectionism?   **SP**

HIGH   What about toward spiritual perfectionism?   HIGH

Brainstorm a moment, and list all the ways you try to be perfect. You might make your list *earthly* and *spiritual*.

Does someone else's perfectionism, either earthly or spiritually, drive you just a little crazy? If so, how?

LOW   For laughs, do you think you're driving anyone crazy? If so, who?   LOW

If you believe you can lose your salvation, I highly encourage you to do an in-depth study on grace and law through the Book of Galatians.

ADDITIONAL READING:
Lord, I Need Grace to Make It Today

KAY ARTHUR

Below read Ephesians 1:1-6 in both the HCSB and The Message versions. As you read, underline phrases and note in the margin ways this passage counters the idea of spiritual perfectionism.

HCSB

1 Paul, an apostle of Christ Jesus by God's will: To the saints and believers in Christ Jesus at Ephesus.

2 Grace to you and peace from God our Father and the Lord Jesus Christ.

3 Praise the God and Father of our Lord Jesus Christ, who has blessed us in Christ with every spiritual blessing in the heavens

4 For He chose us in Him, before the foundation of the world, to be holy and blameless in His sight. In love

5 He predestined us to be adopted through Jesus Christ for Himself, according to His favor and will, to the praise of His glorious grace that He favored us with in the Beloved.

THE MESSAGE

1 I, Paul, am under God's plan as an apostle, a special agent of Christ Jesus, writing to you faithful Christians in Ephesus.

2 I greet you with the grace and peace poured into our lives by God our Father and our Master, Jesus Christ.

3 How blessed is God! And what a blessing he is! He's the Father of our Master, Jesus Christ, and takes us to the high places of blessing in him.

4 Long before he laid down earth's foundations, he had us in mind, had settled on us as the focus of his love, to be made whole and holy by his love.

5 Long, long ago he decided to adopt us into his family through Jesus Christ. (What pleasure he took in planning this!)

6 He wanted us to enter into the celebration of his lavish gift-giving by the hand of his beloved Son.

Describe your biggest struggle in believing God has truly chosen you.

In preparation for this Bible study, I threw the original manuscript before a focus group of twenty-something age women. I gave them full authority to pick the material apart. From their personal stories, struggles, constructive criticism, suggestions, and encouragement I was humbled and greatly equipped. I loved hearing them process the material and talk about their own personal journeys with the Lord. **Most amazing was that all agreed on one thing. Every last one of them struggles to find rest in God.**

What does 2 Corinthians 5:21 tell us Jesus did for us?

For what result did He become sin for us?

Ah, what rest our souls can find in the righteousness of Christ. Jesus was perfect on our behalf. What if today we laid back in God's ardent "choosing and pursuing" of us and exhaled a glorious breath?

I bid you to lay down your Bible study and do it now.

"Jesus wants to free us from working so hard. A deep understanding of grace relieves spiritual perfectionism."
—Tammie

WEEKLY SESSION ANNOUNCEMENTS

Begin familiarizing yourself with Confidence Booster 1
and the Scripture Premise. See the memory cards on page 161.

———————

Start asking God for opportunities to share the
truths you are learning.

———————

Go back and look over the Suggested Service Opportunities at
lifeway.com/tammiehead Have you considered how you might plan on
being the hands and feet of Christ in someone's life while doing this study?
If so, what do you think you or your group will do?

———————

Our Insecurities

Pitfall 2

Satan is outwitting us by using insecurity against us. When Satan attacked Eve, it didn't surprise him when she suddenly didn't know what to believe. Neither does it surprise him when we don't know the truth. He's still attacking, and we're still being thrown for a loop.

One significant way Satan is assaulting us nowadays is through mass media. I'd venture to say that nothing is more traumatizing to our security as women than this. Living free from a chronic state of discontent is nearly unfathomable when we're constantly being told we need to buy more, do more, and be more.

For instance, let's talk about magazines. One look at a cover and the confusion begins. You read, "6 Easy Steps to a Thinner You!" and suddenly you're feeling fat. What's wild is when their content contradicts itself. Like the ones with bikini-clad women portraying perfect bodies, only to feature an article suggesting that we need higher self-esteem. How's that for an oxymoron?

Consider the July 2010 issue of *allure* magazine that proclaimed **39 Confidence Boosters.** When I stumbled on it, I was dumbfounded. Since I already coined the phrase "Confidence Boosters" for our Bible study, the pink and white blurb on the cover seized my attention. As I poured through its pages not only was *allure's* advice shallow but also proved my personal assumptions. Beloved, the heartbeat of consumerism beats after humanity's deep insecurity. And it shouldn't surprise us that our enemy's does too.

Name the last magazine you purchased.

What enticed you to buy it?

BEGIN DRENCHING YOUR MIND WITH CONFIDENCE BOOSTER 1 AND SCRIPTURE PREMISE EPHESIANS 1:4

POTENTIAL IDEAS:

write on your bathroom mirror

inside your running shoes

on a sticky-note attached to your computer screen

in the front of your planner

on your supplement bottles

next to your coffeemaker

set as a reminder on your cell phone

Which suggestion might you take first?

My dear mentor, Beth Moore, wrote a painful and profound book on our common source of torment. *So Long, Insecurity* is painful because it forces you to get honest about your insecurities. Just a few chapters in and you recognize you have a serious problem. But it's also profound in that unlike magazines that suggest shallow solutions, Beth offers an answer that's attainable. We don't need a new exercise program or the hottest trends of the day. We need Jesus. In Him alone do we find true rest for our souls. Only in Him do we stop our toiling. Nothing from the outside will ever bring us the security we're longing for.

We're all terribly fractured with insecurity. Sin has left us in this state, and the enemy plays on it constantly. Satan's goal is to keep believers:

- too self-absorbed to read God's Word and pray
- too busy and distracted with other people's opinions of us
- constantly comparing ourselves and setting unrealistic goals we know we can't keep
- embarrassed by how much we need to grow spiritually but too busy chasing our tails to change anything

If Satan succeeds, he's got a marvelous concoction: a woman God could use mightily to change her world for His glory but who is too caught up with changing or hating herself to know God's marvelous plan for her life.

The core of our problem is we're terribly insecure. Insecure about who God is. Insecure about who we are. Insecure about how God wants us to walk with Him. Insecure about whether we're doing a good enough job. Insecure about feeling like God's shelved us. Insecure about other people's gifting in light of our own. Truly, we're just insecure.

Out of all the areas I just named, which ones best describe your insecurities?

Los Angeles, California, is such a crazy place to drive compared to Houston. Have you been there? We recently visited and happily packed our GPS beforehand. We've nicknamed our GPS *Sheila* since she gives our directions in a fun Australian accent. Only this time Sheila kept us lost. Finally, after much frustration we turned her off and used our iPhone™ maps instead.

I wonder if you have a Sheila? I'm not talking about a GPS named Sheila. I'm talking about a Sheila who beckons you away from your identity in Christ. She's obsessed with giving directions. For some of us, she suggests a counterfeit version of God's will for our lives. Soon our heads are spinning with thoughts such as, *Nothing is really working or changing anyway. Aren't you sick of this God thing? Look. So-and-so doesn't walk with God and things are wonderful for her.* For others, Sheila works in opposite ways. She says, "Wow, you are such a mess. Don't you think it's time you worked a little harder? Got your game on? Look. So-and-so has it all together. Why can't you?"

What does your Sheila say to you?

Consider starting a conversation with a friend this week on this topic.

Who is the ultimate Sheila? How is he described in the following verses?

Revelation 12:10
Job 1:9-11
1 Peter 5:8-9

How did Eve respond when the ultimate Sheila, Satan, came after her (Gen. 3:1-6)?

From the text, whom was Satan really accusing?

Can you identify any correlation between Satan accusing God and your own struggles to believe what God has spoken? What seems similar? While interviewing women for this Bible study, I found they shared disturbing similarities in their insecurities with the Lord. Here are some things I heard:

"Sometimes I don't sense God's presence very much."

"My prayer life could use some help. I don't always feel like God listens when I pray."

"I feel like I am a disappointment to God."

"God has much bigger things to worry about than me."

"I feel really far away from God and disconnected sometimes."

"It's hard to believe God loves me for me."

"I don't understand why He's making me wait. I have a hard time trusting God's heart. I know He's good, but sometimes it feels like He doesn't care."

Can you relate to any of these women? If so, how?

How do you think the ultimate Sheila leads to feelings like these?

Girl, we've got to know God for ourselves. We must come to a place where we can say, "You know what? That is not my God. The way I'm feeling is not my God. That's not my God's voice going on in my head. That's not God's voice in my heart. That's not the way my God thinks toward me. That is not what my God would say to me. My God doesn't feel that way about me." Knowing our God intimately helps us sort through and correct all these false thoughts in our heads.

Did you know the word "accuses" (Rev. 12:10) is a present active participle that basically means again and again and again? Therefore, what should we do again and again and again (1 Pet. 5:8-9)?

Adam and Eve's genesis story has much to teach us about our security in Christ, since it tells how we originally lost both earthly and eternal security. If you're anything like me, then perhaps you do a whole lot better if you know where something is coming from—not that it's always our answer, but sometimes I'm halfway to better just by having that little slice.

Satan is a deceiver. His greatest seduction, over your life and mine, is killing, stealing, and destroying our affection for Christ. He hounds after our insecurities like a ravenous wolf on prey, looking for any possible opening to break our allegiance and obedience to Christ.

Read Genesis 3:1-9. Watch how Satan came after Adam and Eve's security with the Lord.

What were Satan's specific tactics?

How did he twist God's words?

Can you think of a time when Satan twisted God's words to deceive you, causing a deep wound of insecurity? If so, please share.

Beloved, we need a profound revelation of the love of God and a fuller understanding of His character. Our soul-deep beliefs have everything to do with how well we handle daily seductions to insecurity and the accusations Satan brings.

Scores of us, if asked, would say we know the love of God, but do we really?
Here are some questions we can ask ourselves to bring a more accurate answer:

1. Does it seem like God loves you more when you pray, read your Bible, do mission work, keep up with your quiet times, act like a good Christian girl, watch your swearing, stay away from certain people or go to church?
2. Do you constantly feel as if you should be doing more spiritually—as if you can't do enough?
3. Do you oftentimes feel like a failure and rip yourself apart?

If you answered yes to any of those questions, it's time you drink deeper of who God really is. Because this is the deal: How we see God directly impacts how we see ourselves.

Want to see God as He is? Then look at what the psalmist David penned about God.

Read Psalm 145:8-9,13-20 and finish the seven "The LORD" statements from the passages:

(v. 8) The LORD ...

(v. 9) The LORD ...

(v. 13) The LORD ...

(v. 14) The LORD ...

(v. 17) The LORD ...

(v. 18) The LORD ...

(v. 20) The LORD ...

Considering each description, does this sound like the same God you've been envisioning? Explain.

Take some time to talk with the Lord about this now. Practice resting in the heart of your God. Imagine yourself being embraced by every one of those qualities of His character.

Go back and read Genesis 3:7-10,21-24 while specifically looking for the heart of God.

_____

What do you see?

Would you say you envision God this way on most days?

I've read that Genesis passage many times, and the love of God still stuns me. Truth is, God could have waited and let them wallow in the self-loathing of their guilt. After all, you know the familiar saying, "You've made your bed; now lie in it." God could've walked away in total disgust and distanced Himself completely—making Adam and Eve beg, plead, and writhe for forgiveness. But God didn't do any of those things. Why? Because He's not that way.

Restoration of intimacy was no afterthought to God. He'd planned for the whole thing. Hidden here is a powerful truth that has the potential to revolutionize our thinking today: God is not looking for a cleaned-up version of us. He's just looking for us. No pretense. No game face. No Miss Perfect. Just plain, 'ole, ordinary you and me.

Compare the following Scriptures. As you read, circle the words in each verse that indicate exactly when God planned His relationship with you.

Ephesians 1:4
"For He chose us in Him, before the foundation of the world, to be holy and blameless in His sight."

Matthew 25:34
"Then the King will say to those on His right, 'Come, you who are blessed by My Father, inherit the kingdom prepared for you from the foundation of the world.'"

Revelation 13:8
"All those who live on the earth will worship him, everyone whose name was not written from the foundation of the world in the book of life of the Lamb who was slaughtered."

Do you have any "before" areas that are desperate for the truth that God chose you with full knowledge of every decision you would make? He still chose you—before you were talked into getting in that bed, before your heart was broken, before you made promises you wouldn't keep. God chose you before you got scared and ran the other way in rebellion. Before you took matters in your own hands and tried to control things.

Do you have a particular "before"? If so, have you allowed Jesus to fully heal it?

Long before He fashioned your being and breathed His life into yours, God calculated your sinfulness and the sacrifices He'd make. None of it took God by surprise. God chose you, in fact, to redeem you.

What were Adam and Eve doing when God came looking for them (Gen. 3:8)?

Have you ever hidden from God? If so, when and why?

God desires to deliver us from our hiding. Could our fears, doubts, worries, and constant condemnation actually be ways we hide from God without even knowing? Makes perfect sense to me since each keeps us from being with God.

You and I are safe to live in the wide-open with our God and here's why:

Where exactly did Adam and Eve hide from God (Gen. 3:8)?

_____

in the bushes   in the trees   in the flowers

In the margin is 1 Peter 2:24. What is the cross specifically called?

How would you explain to a friend that Adam and Eve's decision to hide in the trees illustrates humanity's need to hide in the cross of Christ?

"He Himself bore our sins in His body on the tree, so that, having died to sins, we might live for righteousness; by His wounding you have been healed."
1 PETER 2:24

Jesus did not die to make us good rule followers. He died to forgive our sin. To minister to our shame. To restore our identity. To make us new. And to empower us to live a life in newfound freedom (Col. 1:20).

The cross of Christ is our hiding place where we should live all our days, saturated in the crazy, wonderful, magnificent love of God.

Which areas of your life need to be better hidden in the cross of Christ?

Pitfall 3

Our Fear

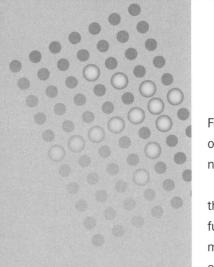

What reason did Adam give God for hiding (Gen. 3:10)?

Fear is such a seizing force, isn't it? Have you noticed how fear does opposing things in your life? One minute you're motivated by it, and the next you're paralyzed. Crazy, huh?

Adam and Eve were so consumed with fear they honestly thought they could hide from God. Fear causes us to do some insane and even funny things sometimes. How about breaking into a full-blown sweat making sure your house is perfect before the arrival of guests? And then answering the door with elevated breathing and dewy skin? What in the world is that about? Fear.

Can you think of a time when fear motivated you to do something funny or embarrassing? If so, explain.

What are you most afraid of lately? Have you handed your fears over to the Lord?

Can you imagine what it was like for Adam and Eve to feel the initial rush of negative emotions? Talk about overwhelming! Here were two people who lived in the eternal, wonderful bliss of God with not a worry or care in the world. Do you suppose this is why they didn't fear Satan's seduction when they should have? Who knows? Regardless, I cannot imagine how sickened they must have felt.

If given the chance, how would you have encouraged Adam and Eve?

Is it hard to believe those same words in your own fearful seasons? If so, why?

In the margin what does Hebrews 4:16 tell us we can always do?

What will we always find?

> "Therefore let us approach the throne of grace with boldness, so that we may receive mercy and find grace to help us at the proper time."
>
> **HEBREWS 4:16**

In Hebrews 4:16 the word for "boldness" actually suggests having a freedom in speaking. What if we quit allowing our fears to consume us and turn every bit of that emotion over to God in prayer? Boldness or confidence is *parresia* and means "Freedom in speaking all one thinks … which manifests itself in confident praying."[4] Maybe it's time we quit being so fearful and start being prayerful with some very specific and even bold requests.

To me the fundamental part of Hebrews 4:16 is approaching. God has reached out to us through the cross. Are we courageous enough to reach back? This is something we must decide daily, and Hebrews 4:16 provides the way. Carefully read the verse in the Amplified Version:

Hebrews 4:16

"Let us then fearlessly and confidently and boldly draw near to the throne of grace (the throne of God's unmerited favor to us sinners), that we may receive mercy [for our failures] and find grace to help in good time for every need [appropriate help and well-timed help, coming just when we need it]."

How do you think God's grace and mercy help when we're afraid?

Sister, have you heard the true meaning of *mercy?* Personally, it's one of my all-time favorite original-language Bible words—maybe because I've needed so much of it.

Read the definition of the Greek word translated *mercy.* **Circle what you consider the most important words or phrases.**

Mercy *"most often involves the expression of pity, the action taken out of compassion for others in which one undertakes to alleviate their misery and relieve their suffering. Mercy is any act which attempts to address compassionately the plight and wretchedness of others. ... it is God's tender regard for the misery of man consequent to sin, and entails all that He performs to alleviate man's plight and remove the curse of sin."* [5]

Do you need to receive a fresh dose of God's mercy? If so, cry out for it by writing a prayer below.

Girlfriend, embrace your inheritance as the daughter of a merciful King. He is solidly yours. Come out of hiding and be caught in His magnificent and wonderful grace. You have been chosen by God before the foundation of the world to be blameless in His sight. No longer does the sinful nature define you; neither should you toil for God's love anymore. **Fall back and rest in the arms of the One who lavishly and unashamedly pursues you for His own.**

Our Shame

Worthlessness vexed much of my young life. Not until my mid-twenties did God begin setting me free. Feelings of worthlessness so warped my identity that I believed insignificance and uselessness described me. God's Word and counseling finally pulled me from that debilitating gutter.

What seemed to seize Adam and Eve when they sinned? (Compare Gen. 2:25 and Gen. 3:10.)

Their disobedience resulted in immediate shame. "Shame springs from fear of others' disgust, disappointment, or ridicule once they know."[6] It is also described as the "devastating effects of sin on the very core of our being," and "a psychological or emotional consequence that flows from guilt and sin."[7] *Vine's Expository Dictionary* says shame has "overtones of being or feeling worthless."[8]

Does that word *worthless* sting? Have you struggled with feelings of worthlessness? If so, how have these feelings affected you?

How are you doing with Confidence Booster 1 and Ephesians 1:4?

—

Can you quote them from memory?

—

Have you shared them yet?

—

If so, with whom and how?

—

Adam and Eve have plenty to teach us about the heart of God. God was not a heavenly policeman throwing His weight around and anxiously waiting to write them a ticket. Nor did He treat them as worthless beings, sinners who should feel ashamed.

How does Hebrews 4:15 particularly describe Jesus' attitude toward us?

○ frusrated   ○ weary   ○ apathetic   ◉ sympathetic

If we predominately hear God speak to us in corrective terms, we need a new view of God. He is not the scary policeman in the sky, watching to see if we break the rules. He is a gentle, sympathetic, loving Father who lavishes us in His grace.

Sometimes we rebel and require loving correction, but we never need to feel worthless, as sinners ashamed before an overbearing Father. If we see God this way, we need to invite Him to come and change our perceptions of Him so they will line up with the God of Scripture. The prophet Joel told us what God says about shame.

In the margin, read God's promise to Joel (Joel 2:26-27).

When Adam and Eve took Satan's bait, shame began to define all who open their lungs to oxygen. But our God is a restorer. Getting this is critical. If we do not see ourselves as valuable to God and valuable before God, then we will never find confidence before Him. Serving Him will always be a duty rather than the delight He intends for us.

Shame is not just a sense of embarrassment. Shame is the personal imprint sin has left on our souls. It tells you you're not good enough in the worst of ways. Shame hits you when you walk into a situation and an inferiority complex seizes you.

Are you ready for this? Shame is your sinful nature testifying of its own character. Yes, apart from God you and I really are not good enough.

**Do you ever feel you're not good enough?
If so, what triggers promote it?**

"My people will never again be put to shame. You will know that I am present in Israel and that I am Yahweh your God, and there is no other. My people will never again be put to shame."

JOEL 2:26-27

In Romans 7 we find the apostle Paul having a real internal battle. If you ever thought he was spiritually perfect, then you'll be quite surprised. He was human just like the rest of us. Deep down, he honestly wanted to make godly choices, but he felt powerless.

Read Romans 7:15-25. What did Paul do in reaction to his feelings (vv. 24-25)?

Were Paul's reactions similar or different than yours? How?

Some additional Scriptures for calling on the Lord:

Acts 2:21;

Psalms 17:6-7; 86:7;

Jeremiah 33:3

Paul's sudden jolt of realization that it wasn't him but sin's existence in him is powerful and profound. His feelngs did not define him as a person. He recognized he could be rescued from how he was feeling.

Paul saw a war within his members—a war with his sinful nature. He realized his job was not to save himself but to call on the Lord.

If self-condemnation has been your bag, you have a promise from Romans 7:15-21. You're not worthless. You don't have to be stuck feeling good for nothing. The Jesus our brother Paul called on to rescue him is the same Jesus who will rescue you. Let's walk together toward the goal of throwing off every hint of shame and worthlessness.

Compare Paul with Adam and Eve. What did Adam and Eve do differently (Gen. 3:7)?

Have you wished you had someone else's fig leaves? How has that worked out for you?

Don't think for a second that we don't do the same. Unless we're crying out for some God kind of help, we're probably sewing fig leaves. In modern days we sew fig leaves such as performance, perfection, control, anger, or passive aggression. Anything that keeps us seeking approval, identity, and self-worth apart from God is a fig leaf.

FIG LEAVES **RESULTS**

In the margin list ways you've sewn fig leaves. To the right of each, explain how they've left you defeated.

We don't need to cover ourselves. Each one of us is already God's favorite–handpicked and loved. Let's be brave and start coming to Him, like the old hymn says, "Just As I Am." Jesus has us completely covered. Next week we will look into this more, but for now I want you to lie back and rest in God's lavish love for you. Still yourself before Him and blessedly receive. You are one step closer from duty to delight. **Ah, yes. You are chosen.**

wrapping things up

A FEW LAST QUESTIONS

1. Can you describe in simple terms what A. W. Tozer called the doctrine of prevenient grace (p. 14)? How will you now actively live as God's chosen and choose to rest in His love?

2. How is your perception of God changing from duty to delight?

3. When life delivers a blow to your confidence, how will you now reconcile it with God's heart?

4. How did memorizing your Confidence Booster and Scripture Premise help you this week?

As God's Chosen, Know Your Rights!

1. **You have the right to enjoy being God's daughter.**
2. **You have the right to face Him fearless and shameless.**
3. **You have the right to come to Him anywhere, anyplace, anytime.**

Consider doing a word study in Scripture on the word chosen. www.blueletterbible.org or www.mystudybible.com are great free online resources. Here are a few verses to get you started: Deuteronomy 7:6; Isaiah 43:10; Colossians 3:12; 1 Peter 2:4.

1. A. W. Tozer, *The Pursuit of God* (Camp Hill, PA: Wing Spread Publishers, 1982), 11.

2. Ibid., 12.

3. Danielle Pergament, "39 Confidence Boosters" in *allure* magazine (July 2010).

4. Spiros Zodhiates, gen. ed., *Key Word Study Bible* (Chattanooga, TN: AMG International, Inc., 1996), 1660.

5. Ibid., 1619.

6. Lawrence O. Richards, *The Teacher's Commentary* (Wheaton, IL: Scripture Press Publications, Inc., 1983), 988.

7. Leland Ryken, James C. Wilhoit, Tremper Longman III, gen. eds., *Dictionary of Biblical Imagery* (Downer's Grove, IL: IVP Academic, 1998), 780.

8. W. E. Vine, *Vine's Complete Expository Dictionary* (Nashville, TN: Thomas Nelson Publishers, 1996), 339.

....

Father, thank You for all You've taught me this week. Your grace and mercy on my life is nothing short of astounding. It means so much to know I can rest in Your choosing of me. I do not have to work for Your love. All I have to do is receive it. Please continue to teach me how to receive Your love better. I truly want to learn how to stay drenched in You. In Jesus' name I pray. Amen.

....

Knowing God Has
Redeemed Us

Two cavernous hungers tug at the human soul—hungers for acceptance and for satisfaction. We all have stories of trying to placate these hungers—some painful tales and some embarrassing. This week will we hear three words of advice to fill our God-given hungers for acceptance and satisfaction. Will we listen? The choice is ours to make.

I Am Redeemed

Scripture Premise:

"We have redemption in Him through His blood, the forgiveness of our trespasses, according to the riches of His grace that He lavished on us with all wisdom and understanding."

Ephesians 1:7-8

First Word of Advice:
Eat More Bread

Second Word of Advice:
Drink More Blood

Third Word of Advice:
Remember Your Redemption

·WEEKLY SESSION ANNOUNCEMENTS

Begin familiarizing yourself with Confidence Booster 2 and your Scripture Premise.

Don't let up reciting Confidence Booster 1 and Ephesians 1:4.

Start asking God for opportunities to share the truths you are learning.

How's your service opportunity going? Have you served anyone yet?

Be prepared to reflect on communion later this week by purchasing bread and juice.

First Word of Advice:

Eat More Bread

For the last several years, our family has gone to Zambia, Africa, to love on orphans. The ministry we serve alongside feeds the children plenty of bread. I've watched the simplicity of bread bring profound satisfaction and peace to children with starving bellies and aching hearts. **My experience there always makes me question: "Do I hunger for the Bread of life with the same desperation as these children hunger for physical bread?"**

Ponder this question, and write your thoughts.

This week we will meddle in the lives of a handful of people: Adam and Eve, the Israelites, and those Jesus encountered in the New Testament. We plan to take one more step from duty toward delight by grasping a significant feature of our multifaceted redemption. **Christ has come, through the bread of His body, to supply our hunger for satisfaction with a feast on the bread of His Presence.**

What first command did God give (Gen. 2:16-17)?

Compare God's words with the enemy's temptation in Genesis 3:1-5. How do God's words and the enemy's temptation both ultimately center on satisfying hunger?

In what ways was Eve looking for satisfaction apart from God (Gen. 3:6)?

Here we see the age-old dilemma and temptation of trying to meet our need for satisfaction apart from God. Thousands of years may separate us from Eve, but the temptation to dine on something other than God's Word remains. Eve was caught in the trap of finding the desirable apart from God. Throughout Scripture we repeatedly see God's creation in this predicament. From Adam and Eve to the Israelites and all the way up to you and me, our struggle is the same.

Did you notice that Satan stressed the negative while God's command was first positive? Beware of seeking satisfaction through denial alone.

HOW WOULD YOU RATE YOUR DAILY DEPENDENCE ON GOD TO SATISFY YOU?

1   2   3   4   5   6   7   8   9   10

(Need some help!)   (Doing good!)

Think of your relational history with Jesus. When have you relied on Him least for satisfaction? Most? Why? I'll provide you with a couple of examples.

Least: When I liked a guy.

Why? I'd get distracted in the validation a guy brings and the possibility of marriage.

Most: When I thought I would lose my job.

Why? It scared me, and I ran to God.

Looking for satisfaction apart from God assails us all. We look for it in positions we hold, places we live, vehicles we drive, addictions we practice, brands we wear, and knowledge we possess. All idolatry and disobedience come from looking for satisfaction apart from Christ.

How did Jesus handle Satan's temptation to satisfy His hunger apart from God (Luke 4:1-4)?

Satan tempted Jesus to use His power for turning the stone into what?

○ water　　　○ honey　　　○ bread　　　○ meat

When Jesus answered Satan with, "It is written: Man must not live on bread alone" (v. 4), He was quoting Deuteronomy 8:3. Before we turn there, let's build a foundation so we'll have a greater appreciation for why Jesus quoted that text.

The Israelites had been in Egyptian captivity for 400 years and groaned for God to deliver them. God responded to their cry because of His covenant (Ex. 2:23-25; 3:7-8). He called Moses to lead the people. With much drama, God freed His people from captivity and sent them on their way to Canaan, the land flowing with milk and honey. Before they arrived, something interesting happened in the desert.

God answered the Israelites' request for freedom from slavery, but what did they do only a little after their rescue (Ex. 16:1-3)?

Why were they grumbling?

For what were they asking?

Do you think this could be a satisfaction issue? If so, how?

Have you ever cried out for God to set you free and then—when He did—you grumbled over His process? If so, what were the circumstances?

Only a month had passed since the Israelites left Egypt. My Holman Christian Standard Bible comments, 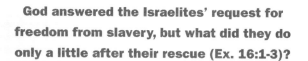"The people's memory was short and their hearts ungrateful."[1] Has that ever been me! Many times I've begged God to set me free and then balked at His process. Usually my complaint is just that—the process. I'd rather have fast freedom instead of slow freedom. Like my friend's toddler who hollers his head off if you don't shovel the food in fast enough, I want freedom, and I want it now.

I long for instant satisfaction. I suspect you do too.

Do we really want freedom as badly as we think?

What does Exodus 16:4 say God did in response to their need and to their complaints?

(See Ex. 16:4-15 for more of the story.)

_____

○ fed them anyway   ○ punished them harshly
○ struck them dead   ○ shut His ears

What did God use to satisfy their hunger?

Other than your salvation, can you think of a time when God rained blessings on you when you obviously didn't deserve them?

Concerning the journey from Egypt to Canaan, the *Key Word Study Bible* says: "The Lord did not take the Israelites to Canaan by the most direct route. The people needed not only to observe His mighty works, but also to learn to depend upon Him for the necessities of life. Ultimately, they needed to understand that all would be accomplished by God's own power and not by their own ability. ... God was teaching them that even though they had been brought out of bondage and had witnessed the defeat of the Egyptian army, they must still depend upon Him."[2]

Often we fail to recognize that waiting forces desperation. When we are desperate, we become willing to listen to whatever God says. God considers the lapse of time between slavery and freedom critical. He patiently waits for us to be convinced of His faithfulness because "faith is being sure of what we hope for and certain of what we do not see" (Heb. 11:1, NIV).

Recall a season when God did not take you down the easier route. What lessons might you have missed if given a quicker, easier path?

Are you perhaps there again? Is it time to give up the fight and comply? If so, what would that look like?

In biblical times bread was a daily dietary staple. By the time children were old enough to handle solid foods, their mothers were adding bread to their daily meal portions. A Hebrew family had no time for picky eaters. You ate bread, and you had a mind to like it. If the ancients visited our day with all our breadless diets, they'd think we'd lost our marbles.

Read Deuteronomy 8:1-10, and fill in the rest of verse 3:

"so that you might _make you know_
that man does not _live_ on
bread alone but on every _word_
that comes from the mouth of the LORD."

Considering the Israelites and God's lesson with the bread from heaven, read John 6:48-58.

the bread of life

What did Jesus call Himself?

How does this passage support the advice: Eat More Bread?

For further reflection read John 6:1-59. Similarities to the Israelites in Exodus abound. "John presents a thoroughgoing development of the metaphor of hunger. With clear reference to the experience of Israel in the wilderness, Jesus not only provides food for the crowd (Jn 6:1-14), but describes Himself as the Bread of life meeting spiritual as well as physical needs (Jn 6:31-58)."[3]

Several days ago I pulled out my journal and read to my oldest, Peyton, an encouraging word God had spoken over my heart from the Holy Scriptures earlier that day. She knew I was working through a particular fear, and it was so fun to tell her how God had encouraged my heart. I want so much for my girls to know what it's like to live on the very words of God and to experience the rich satisfaction it brings to the depths of our being. Sister, I want this for you too.

When Jesus entered that wilderness, it was the Holy Spirit who led Him there. Nothing about it was haphazard or accidental. It was a test—a test to see whether Jesus would rely completely on His Father. After 40 days of hunger no less. Can you even imagine?

The beauty of Jesus is that He accomplished in 40 short days all that man could not. What took the Israelites 40 years to learn, Jesus completed in a span of six weeks. Ironically, that's the same amount of time as our Bible study.

Compare Luke 4:1 with 4:14 in the margin.

In reference to the Spirit, how did Jesus enter and exit the wilderness?

If we are Christians, you and I will never enter a wilderness experience without the presence of God's Spirit. He comes to live inside of us the moment of salvation. We'll talk more about this in week 3. We can experience a vast difference, however, in how we leave those wilderness places. When we rely on God and His truth as our sole sufficiency, we come out in the power of the Spirit.

Sometimes life isn't working for us because God is stirring a holy dissatisfaction. He wants us to want Him more. He allows and even creates wilderness places in our lives to shake us from our apathies and lukewarm conditions. Why? Because **God created us for satisfaction, and He knows we are most happy when we are most satisfied by Him.**

This past weekend I had the privilege to go into a suspected brothel to share Christ with a woman. Repeatedly she said, "I'm so empty. I'm so empty." Her sister had been hit by a car and lay in a coma at a local hospital. This traumatic event rocked her from any sense of satisfaction. She became aware of her own unrelenting fear of not knowing her eternal destiny. I saw a woman utterly overwhelmed with dissatisfaction. I also saw peace fill her face when she dropped to her knees and accepted Christ.

"Then Jesus returned from the Jordan, full of the Holy Spirit, and was led by the Spirit in the wilderness."
LUKE 4:1

"Then Jesus returned to Galilee in the power of the Spirit, and news about Him spread throughout the entire vicinity."
LUKE 4:14

What circumstance has God used to stir dissatisfaction in you?

How much time do you spend daily with the Lord? How might you grow that time?

RECOMMENDED READING

Wilderness Skills for Women

(Nashville, TN: B&H Publishing Group)

MARIAN JORDAN

Beloved, every hunger begins and ends with the sufficiency of Christ.

The first question in the Westminster Shorter Catechism of 1674 asks, "What is the chief end of man?" The answer is: "Man's chief end is to glorify God, and to enjoy him forever."[4]

Have you realized that your chief purpose is to enjoy God? Could I make a suggestion about how to enjoy Him more? I want to challenge you to eat more Bread by consuming larger doses of God's Word. I'm not talking about forcing yourself to read the Bible as a matter of duty. Rather, I mean that as we dine with Jesus on the bread of His Presence He not only sustains us with His life but also satisfies our souls to the depths. If we will devour our Bibles—studying, memorizing, praying, obeying—our hearts will bloom with satisfaction.

Second Word of Advice:
Drink More Blood

My husband has a serious case of poison ivy. The itching is driving him nuts. Although I've never had poison ivy, I know what it's like to have an itch you can't scratch. The need for approval and validation create those kinds of itches. No matter how hard we repeatedly scratch, they return.

Leaping from duty to delight requires understanding something. Not only has God chosen us but He has redeemed us. The multifaceted meaning of redemption scratches our itches. When stated simply, it means God has purchased us from sin by the sacrifice of Jesus' sinless body and blood offered on the cross. **Jesus' very life covers yours and mine, and we stand lavishly approved before a Holy God.**

When I was a baby Christian, I heard a pastor's wife share her morning ritual with Jesus. She toasted a bagel, drank a cup of orange juice, read her Bible, and wrote in a journal. She told us exactly how she prayed. I hung on every word, taking tons of notes.

Guess what I did? The next morning I toasted my bagel, drank my glass of orange juice, read my Bible, and prayed her prayers. Trouble was I'm not an early morning eater, I prefer coffee to juice, and her prayers didn't sound like me at all.

I realized I was looking for approval from God. I didn't understand that God approved of me because of Christ, alone. I also didn't understand that personal worship is unique to our individual personalities and God's work in us.

Some of us have lived in a perpetual state of weariness because we've allowed what our friends do, what our mothers do—perhaps, even what our teachers, preachers, and mentors do—to define what we do. And, it's not working. We're frustrated and defeated.

Consider this conversation I had with a friend:

> **My sweet friend:** I feel so bad that I don't get down on my knees and pray before I go to bed. I just feel like I am supposed to, and I feel so guilty because a lot of times I am tired and I want to get in the bed.
> **Me:** Who told you that you have to do that? Did God tell you to do that?
> **Her:** No.
> **Me:** Does someone you know and look up to do that?
> **Her:** Yes.
> **Me (in passionate volume):** Stop comparing yourself to her, and go to bed!

You should have seen my friend's eyes when I said that. It was as if I had smacked her. But God set her free.

Reflect on and write this week's Confidence Booster and Scripture Premise.

What about you? How would you finish the following sentence? "I feel so bad that I don't _____ _____**."**

I would lovingly say to you what I said to her, "Who told you that you have to do that? Did God tell you? Or does someone you look up to do that?" Depending on your answer, I'd be inclined to say, "Girlfriend, you had better obey God, or stop comparing!"

The problem with comparing is we're not wired the same as everyone else. What works for one person doesn't work for another. And that's OK. If God isn't the inspiration for doing what we do, let's abandon those man-made expectations and run to the cross. What we're ultimately looking for is approval, and because Jesus offered His life for us, we already have it.

Beloved, it's time we crawled up into our Savior's lap and receive His lavish acceptance.

It's time we quit trying so hard.
It's time we relent of questioning God's motives.
It's time we identify with Jesus' sacrifices for us.
It's time we fully believe in Jesus' forgiveness.
It's time we renounce trying to surrender and just do it.
It's time we put an end to resisting God and begin resting in Him.
It's time we dump what we're not and reach for who God is.
It's time we plant our feet firmly on God's promises.
It's time you and I delight in God.
Maybe it's time we type this out and tape it to our mirrors
to remind us: It's time.

Which "It's time" statement represents you best right now?

Or if you wrote your own what would you say?

I hope I'm not wearing you out with Adam and Eve. But to appreciate God's second word of advice, Drink More Blood, we must return to the beginning displays of redemption.

Please read Genesis 3:7-21. Imagine you are an innocent bystander (no pun intended) engrossed in this whole scene, like a car wreck you can't help but watch. Here's a little something for you creatives and noncreatives alike: **use verses 7 and 21 to relay the sights you are seeing and the feelings you are feeling.**

Did this little practice make your emotions
as tender as it did mine? If so, how?

The slaying and skinning of an animal is gruesome. Yet this bloody and gruesome situation symbolized, pictured, and predicted God's future plan. He was forging a much greater reality on that garden soil—the reality of redemption.

What does 1 Peter 1:18-19 say we've been redeemed by?
○ silver   ○ precious blood of Christ
○ our forefathers   ○ gold

According to Leviticus 17:11, why is blood so precious?

What actually covers your life?

**How does the prophecy of Christ in
Isaiah 53:4-12 confirm all this?**

Oh, the thought that the sweet life of God covers you and me. Talk about love so amazing.

Blood has an incredible startle factor for us moderns, doesn't it? Whether it's freaking out a mama whose son just fell off the bed and busted his mouth open or a child being fine after she's fallen only to discover a bloody knee … let the drama begin. Nope. We do not like blood.

Funny About Our Family

When we're in the car,
Peyton, Savannah, and
I have been known to
talk "girl" talk. Yes. It's
exactly what I mean.
The sheer mention of
it makes my husband
green. Which is
exactly why we do it!
Sick humor, I know.

Note this great quote by Paul Brand: "We moderns have an initial resistance to the intrusion of blood into our religion. In this respect, we differ from all previous cultures. Virtually all 'primitive' religions, including those of Rome and Greece, believed blood had sacramental power, and a bloodless religion would have seemed feckless to most ancients. To them, blood was an everyday substance. They killed their calves and chickens with knives before feasting, whereas we moderns select ours in shrink-wrapped packages, drained of blood and all reminder of slaughter."[5]

The rich imagery of Christ's blood throughout God's Word is entirely central to the gospel. If we drain our Christianity of Christ's blood, we shrink-wrap ourselves out of a relationship. We're qualified for any kind of relationship with our Creator only by the blood of Jesus offered on Calvary. Intimacy with God completely depends on His blood. Why? Only the blood makes us acceptable to God, bringing atonement.

Did you notice the word "atonement" in Leviticus 17:11? Do you know what it means? Take a shot at defining it in your own words.

Even those who've grown up in the church and are accustomed to churchy phraseology would probably have trouble defining *atonement* with a good, solid answer. If you struggled and read ahead, you're busted. Can we say overachiever? I'm kidding. I would have done it too.

Scripture uses two different kinds of language to describe what Jesus did for us on the cross. It uses the language of law and the language of sacrificial worship. *Atonement* or *atone* is what scholars call sacrificial language. *Atone (kapar)* means to cover, reconcile, cleanse, forgive.[6] It's actually one of the most important words in the Bible, often used with reference to covering sin with the blood of the sacrifice.

The simplest definition of *atone*? At + one = atone. God knew exactly what He was doing when He exchanged Adam and Eve's covering. He was suggesting the redemptive work of Christ in that His blood and body would cover us, cleanse us, and bring us back into intimate fellowship by making us one again.

Compare Matthew 1:23-24 and Ephesians 2:13-14, looking for suggestions of atonement.

_____

Are you beginning to see God ordained for you and Him to be close? If so, how will you make room for the two of you to get to know each other more?

Last night, after I wrote those words to you, I wrapped up writing because I couldn't stop sobbing. I bowed my head at my computer and found myself profusely apologizing for not loving God the way He deserves. Then, before I knew it, I found myself apologizing on behalf of everyone else in creation who rejects the kindness and love of God.

Have you ever considered the massive rejection God set Himself up for when He created us? What does this stir in your heart?

God's love for us is scandalous. We don't deserve such a loving God. These truths make me want to fall on my face and worship with absolute abandon. What joy to finally gather around heaven's throne, with sin no longer hindering our relationship, and pour forth the excessive adoration due to such a God.

Our humanity dooms our purest efforts. We cannot possibly give back to God what He so extravagantly deserves, but what if we tried? What if gratefulness motivated our obedience above anything else? What if we obeyed not as a way to justify ourselves but purely as a way to bring God pleasure?

Does gratefulness motivate your obedience? Why or why not?

Do you obey as a way to bring God pleasure? If not, why?

Earlier today I ran into the man who led me to Christ. Curtis and his lovely wife Julie loved my lost heart to life in the Lord. Fresh tenderness washes over me every time I see them. They lavished my lost heart with unconditional acceptance, never judging me for my sin. It blew me away when they continued to pursue our relationship because deep in my heart I knew they knew I was not like them. I was darkness, and they were light. I was a sinner, and they were saints. What I saw in these two precious people was the grace of God wrapped in human flesh.

The blood of Jesus covers us with the rich approval of God. We don't have to be perfect. We don't have to spiritually bat 1000. We don't have to know all the answers. The blood of Jesus invites us to stretch out and rest in God because Jesus was perfect for us. He batted 1000 on our behalf. All we have to do is receive.

Take in with fresh wonder the words to the old hymn:

Nothing But the Blood

What can wash away my sin?
Nothing but the blood of Jesus;
What can make me whole again?
Nothing but the blood of Jesus.

Oh! precious is the flow
That makes me white as snow;
No other fount I know,
Nothing but the blood of Jesus.

For my pardon, this I see,
Nothing but the blood of Jesus;
For my cleansing this my plea,
Nothing but the blood of Jesus.

Nothing can for sin atone,
Nothing but the blood of Jesus;
Naught of good that I have done,
Nothing but the blood of Jesus.

This is all my hope and peace,
Nothing but the blood of Jesus;
This is all my righteousness,
Nothing but the blood of Jesus.

"By this will,
we have been sanctified
through the offering of the
body of Jesus Christ once and
for all. ... For by one offering He
has perfected forever those
who are sanctified."

HEBREWS 10:10,14

**What has Jesus' sacrifice done for us?
See Hebrews 10:10,14 in the margin.**

Some translations use "sanctified" and others use "holy" in describing what the sacrifice of Jesus has provided us. Both words mean *set apart*, *consecrated*, *saint* and describe someone who is "set apart from a common to a sacred use."[7]

**How do you feel about being that someone?
about seeing yourself as sacred?**

**How would you be different tomorrow if you
woke up believing you were highly significant
to God and set apart for His purposes?**

I came across an old prayer journal recently, and the pages were stained with tears. Memories flooded my mind and tendered my heart as I thought about the night those tears were shed. I had been crying over how much I hated myself. I knew I had serious issues with how I felt about myself that I couldn't seem to overcome. In desperation I sat before the Lord in my room and cried out for help as I pressed the pen into the paper and wrote as fast as I could.

After I poured out my heart, I opened God's Word. This just happened to be what I saw: "All beautiful, you are my darling; there is no flaw in you" (Song of Songs 4:7, NIV).

Everything in me rejected those words. I found myself sobbing more and repeating the words: "Oh, but there is. That's what You say about me; it's not what I say about me. I'm so flawed."

Do you sometimes feel flawed and have a hard time reconciling your beliefs with God's view of you? If so, how?

Messages that promote self-loathing and self-hate batter us constantly. Just one trip to the grocery store checkout lane makes you want to change yourself or hate yourself. Every magazine shouts thinner, fewer wrinkles, get on a new diet or exercise routine. All those voices scream that we need something more to be acceptable.

How do you deal with messages of insecurity like these?

Should you be buying magazines and watching shows that pressure you to feel flawed? Please don't start thinking I'm the media police. I'm not. I gravitate to the nearest magazine just as you do. But can your heart really handle the feeding of these media messages right now? Sometimes it's critical to fast for some time from certain television shows and magazines to get the healing we need. Not that we can't watch or read them again. We just can't both leave Egypt and take Egypt with us if we want freedom.

How did Christ offer Himself according to Hebrews 9:14?

The *Key Word Study Bible* uses another word for *without blemish*. It uses *flawless*.[8] The Flawless One has covered all of your flaws and mine.

How would you rate your level of daily guilt with the Lord?

not much   **more than I'd like**   **all the time**   **beyond major**

Can you tell the difference between guilt and conviction? If so, how would you explain?

If you said anything about guilt having its origins in shame, you are exactly right. We saw this in Adam and Eve when they hurried to sew their coverings and position themselves behind the tree. Working hard and embarrassed. So, how can we tell the difference between sinful guilt and God-given conviction? Here's a simple piece of advice I use continuously:

GUILT LEADS TO PERFORMANCE   CONVICTION LEADS TO REPENTANCE (a changed mind)

According to 1 John 1:9, what's our response to conviction, and what can we expect?

How does Hebrews 10:19-23 support the same idea?

How would your sin, guilt, and repentance patterns change if you believed this?

Conviction from the Lord is a beautiful gift because it keeps us close to Him. However, guilt, in this context, is a ball and chain. Satan, the ultimate accuser, uses our feelings of guilt to distance us from God.

God has chosen us.
God has covered us with His blood and body.
God has lavished us with His acceptance.

God uses these three facts to break us free from cycles of penance and guilt-driven performance. God is not looking for perfection. Jesus has already been perfect for us. He covered our past sins, present sins, and future sins in the forgiveness of His blood. Accepting Christ's gift should never make us apathetic. It should make us profoundly grateful and provide us delight. Where we bask in our redemption, and Jesus inspires us to Drink More Blood. Why? Because Jesus' blood provides glorious, soul-satisfying approval for all who are willing to drink. Sister, let's lift up our glasses and drink deeply.

Read John 6:53-56 and ponder over Jesus' words.

Third Word of Advice:
Remember Your Redemption

My mother-in-law, Barbara, and her siblings tell of suppertimes around their family table. Their stories always makes me smile. I love that they tell them with the same enthusiasm and joy as if it's their first time.

Their daddy, Eric, was a wonderful man. When they gathered around the table, he insisted the mood be kept lighthearted and fun. All the neighborhood kids loved to eat at the Samms' house. When you asked for a piece of bread, Daddy would send it to you flying.

Today we gather around the table with Jesus and the disciples for the last supper. We're not told of the mood when they first took their places around the table. I'm sure being with Jesus included an air of lightheartedness and fun, but this time it didn't stay that way long. Conversations turned serious and a blowup ensued as Jesus warned of an impending betrayal by someone sitting at the table. Eleven were shocked and appalled, and an argument broke out. They protested, "How could this be? We love you!"

Once again Jesus began to make strange statements similar to "the one who eats My flesh and drinks My blood lives in Me" (John 6:56). This time the subject was bread and wine.

They celebrated the Passover meal with Jesus acting as host. Passover begins at sundown and commemorates the Israelites' deliverance from slavery in Egypt. The observance is the oldest feast continuously celebrated throughout the world. In Exodus 12:17 God commanded, "You are to observe the Festival of Unleavened Bread because on this very day I brought your divisions out of the land of Egypt. You must observe this day throughout your generations as a permanent statute." The disciples were deeply familiar with the ceremony. They repeated it every year of their lives.

Then Jesus put a new spin on the ancient ritual. He said that when they ate the bread and drank the wine, they were to "do this in remembrance of Me" (Luke 22:19).

For the participants these words must have been confusing. Why would they need to remember? Only later would they understand what God had done through Passover. The ancient ritual pictured and paved the way for the sacrifice of Jesus.

To fully explain the meaning of Passover requires multiple volumes, but here's a small taste of the symbolism. God made three key symbolic foods part of the meal (Ex. 12:8). The unblemished lamb pictures innocence. Since yeast (leaven) causes fermentation, it pictures sin. The unleavened bread, called matzah, pictures purification from sin. The bitter herbs remind participants of the bitterness of Egyptian slavery.

Close this segment by writing your Confidence Booster and Scripture Premise. Describe any changes this truth is making in your life.

With those meanings in mind, let's compare the original Passover to the present Passover. **Read Exodus 12:1-7,12-15.**

What was the requirement for the Passover lamb (v. 5)?

How does verse 13 suggest the blood leads to God's acceptance?

Redemption means the sinless Lamb of God was sacrificed on our behalf. We become acceptable to God forevermore. We never have to hide again. His blood has made atonement for our sin, and we can rest in the Lord's amazing grace. The blood of Jesus Christ is our security for perfection. Is this glorious or what? All we can do is trust God and His provisions. In Him we are a flawless, worthy people because God says so.

How do you think the bread of Passover symbolically ties together God's provision of bread in the wilderness and Jesus' declaration that He is the Bread of life?

Nothing in this life will ever bring the satisfaction we're longing for like the presence of Christ. For this time Jesus Christ, the Word who became flesh, lives with us through His Word and His Spirit. He has come with the bread of His body to fill our souls' deepest need for satisfaction (John 1:1,14). We do not have to be like Eve or the Israelites, giving in to the temptation of finding satisfaction apart from God. Jesus, the Bread of life, desires to be the everyday staple for meeting our needs.

Jesus bids you and me to recline in His tender loving care.

Please read Luke 22:14-20. In the following passage taken from the *Dictionary of Biblical Imagery*, underline words or phrases that speak to you about the meaning of the Lord's Supper.

"The Greek word *deipnon*, infrequently translated 'supper,' is usually translated 'banquet,' 'feast' or 'meal' and (meaning especially the main meal of the day). … It occurred at sunset, after the work of the day was finished, and the entire household was present. It was a leisurely meal at which family members and guests conversed at length. It was a time to relax. … Supper to biblical people suggested comparatively abundant food, coming at the end of the working day and thus embodying longing, satisfaction and reward for labor.

"Modern English translations of the Bible generally restrict the use of supper to three major events: Last Supper, Lord's Supper and… supper of the Lamb." In these, you can see "Jesus' lifelong practice of participating in and hosting meals where he demonstrated acceptance by welcoming sinners and outcasts as friends. … The Last Supper … is a meal among former strangers who have become friends, forming a new kind of family with Jesus as head of household."[9]

When Jesus lifted the elements of communion and proclaimed, "Do this in remembrance of Me," He was calling us to heed the advice: Eat More Bread, Drink More Blood, and Remember Your Redemption. Jesus' sacrifice makes you and me—once strangers, outcasts, sinners—now family and friends. Because of Jesus' blood and body we are covered in the grace of God forevermore. We can relax in His presence, enjoying acceptance, satisfaction, and ultimately delight.

The Lord's Supper is a church ordinance to share with your church family. So what I am about to suggest is not full communion in that sense. However, as a celebration of what Jesus has done for you, I bid you to take out the juice and bread and dine with the Lord now. Let the elements physically remind you of His presence. Thank Him that His blood graphically pictures your acceptance and the bread represents His body, given for your satisfaction. Fully recline in His presence with absolute security and freedom. Jesus' atoning sacrifice is your trust.

Finish today by reading Romans 8:31-39.
Write a note to Jesus expressing your feelings.

wrapping things up

A FEW LAST QUESTIONS

1. Can you describe in simple terms what atonement by Jesus' blood means?

2. What is the difference between guilt and conviction?

3. In what ways has your perception of God changed from duty to delight?

4. How did your Confidence Boosters and Scripture Premises help you this week?

As God's Redeemed, Know Your Rights!

1. **Christ accepts you.**
2. **Christ satisfies you.**
3. **You stand before God covered, cleansed, and redeemed.**

1. HCSB Study Bible (Nashville, TN: Holman Bible Publishers, 2010), 126.

2. Spiro Zodhiates, gen. ed., *Key Word Study Bible* (Chattanooga, TN: AMG Publishers, 1996), 87.

3. Leland Ryken, James C. Wilhoit, Tremper Longman III, gen. eds. *Dictionary of Biblical Imagery* (Downers Grove, IL: IVP Academic, 1998).

4. Philip Schaff, *The Creeds of Christendom*, vol. 1 (Grand Rapids, MI: Baker Books, 1984).

5. Paul Brand, "Blood, Part 1: The Miracle of Cleansing" [online] July 2003 [citied 17 January 2011]. Available from the Internet: http://www.christianitytoday.com/ct/2003/julyweb-only/7-7-44.0.html

6. Zodhiates, 1523.

7. Spiros Zodhiates, *The Complete Word Study Dictionary* (Chattanooga, TN: AMG Publishers, 1993), 70.

8. Zodhiates, *Key Word Study Bible*, 1584.

9. Ryken, Wilhoit, Longman, 828.

....

Father, I am astounded by Your covering, cleansing, and fullness of communion with me. Thank You for freeing me from my performances and guilt by lavishing me with Your love. I don't ever want to forget how to live in this place of acceptance and satisfaction with You. Please remind me to take Your advice to Eat More Bread, Drink More Blood, and Remember Your Redemption often. I lay myself down fully at Your feet and rest in Your provision for me. You are my delight. In Jesus' name. Amen.

....

Going from Duty to Delight

THIRD STOP

Knowing God Has
Promised Us

Broken promises. We've all known their sting. Some hurt more than others, but all disappoint. Many of us experience God as duty rather than delight because we've felt that pain and learned to expect more of the same. This week we'll hear a promise out of the mouth of our Redeemer—one we can count on Him to always keep.

I Am Promised

Scripture Premise:

"We have also received an inheritance in Him, predestined according to the purpose of the One who works out everything in agreement with the decision of His will, so that we who had already put our hope in the Messiah might bring praise to His glory."

Ephesians 1:11-12

Six Promises We'll Receive and Stand On

1. God is our faithfulness.
2. God is our transformation.
3. God is our protection, always.
4. God is our Rock.
5. God is our Counselor.
6. God is our inheritance, and we are His.

Promise 1
God Is Our Faithfulness

I hope you are refreshed in knowing that while you were busy grabbing your Bible, your workbook, and perhaps trying to find a decent writing tool, I've thought ahead and offered a prayer for you. **I've asked the Lord to show up in sweet fellowship as you dine with Him through the pages of His unfailing Word.**

Here in our third week we hit a pivotal point. We begin to shift from learning about our security in Christ to ardently taking our stand in His presence. We've been laying a foundation of God's heart toward us. We've saturated ourselves with the truth that God chose to pursue us long before we lost intimacy with Him. He loved us before the creation of the world. We've also seen that God not only pursues us but He also lavishly provides for us by Jesus' cross. His blood and body offer us fullness of acceptance and rich satisfaction.

Looking into the rearview mirror of the course we've charted, we've learned that shame before God is not ours to bear. Nor are discouragement, self-doubt, condemnation, prayerlessness, or confusion for that matter. God has given us a road map that steers us clear. If we do find ourselves in one of those places, we know the way home. Our Confidence Boosters and Scripture Premises point the way.

Recall your Confidence Boosters and cite the Scripture Premises.

1.

2.

3.

As we open our Bibles, the Israelites are our traveling partners once again. This time they're in a total mess. Regardless, God made a promise that eclipsed their disobedience and offered hope. Not just to them. This promise extends to you and me as well.

WEEKLY SESSION ANNOUNCEMENTS

Begin familiarizing yourself with Confidence Booster 3 and your Scripture Premise.

_____

Don't let up reciting Confidence Boosters 1, 2, and Ephesians 1:4,7-8.

_____

Start asking God for opportunities to share with someone the truths you are learning.

_____

Whom have you served this past week? How?

_____

What did the Israelites say to Moses when he read the book of the covenant to them (Ex. 24:7)?

What did Moses sprinkle on the people after their confession (Ex. 24:8)?

Why did Moses sprinkle blood on them?

Moses sprinkled the people with blood because God knew they could not measure up to His righteous requirements of obedience. The blood Moses used pictures the perfect blood of Jesus. **His blood is our only hope for security before a holy God. We cannot keep God's righteous requirements—no matter how hard we try.**

If you suffer from the illusion that you can keep God's law, take a lesson from the Israelites' example. In Jeremiah 32 God confronted them with the facts that they had "done nothing but what is evil in My sight!" (v. 30), turned their backs to God and not their faces (v. 33), placed "detestable things" in God's temple (v. 34), and even burned their own children to the pagan god Molech (v. 35).

Girlfriend, that is some serious rebellion after all God did to save their scrawny necks from Egypt. And after all the patience He expended on them in the Wilderness of Sin? As much as I can think, *What on earth is your problem after all God has done for you?*" I'm soberly reminded I am the very same way. Lord, have mercy on us all.

Have you come to a time when you ceased judging the Israelites and realized you were just like them? If so, what caused your insight?

Now, watch what God did, and tell me it doesn't do something for your soul. In Jeremiah 31 He promised a new covenant with the house of Israel and with the house of Judah (v. 31).

Read Jeremiah 31:33-37, and note the differences God promised in the new covenant.

_____

Where is the new covenant written (v. 33)?

How certain is God's promise of the new covenant (vv. 35-37)?

Describe in your own words what God promised them.

God's knows we're a mess. He knows we cannot and will not do this relationship thing unless He comes and does it in us. Oh, the thought.

You and I make up one big heap of broken promises to God, don't we? Yet He steps forward and says: "I know you can't; that's why 'I will.' Before the foundation of the world, 'I will.' In the garden, 'I will.' Today, 'I will.' I will be your God, and you will be My people."

God Is Our Transformation

When you compare the old covenant God gave Moses to the new covenant God announced through Jeremiah and delivered through Jesus, you will find: "Instead of changing His covenant relationship to his people because they broke the covenant, in his grace, God finds a way whereby they will not break the New Covenant. How can this be done? God will write the law *within* them; *on* their heart he will inscribe it (*emphasis mine*). The Old Covenant had been engraved in stone. The New Covenant will include a revolutionary change in 'will, heart and conscience.' "[1]

The new-covenant promise excels the old-covenant promise because it contains a guarantee of divine intervention and rescue. God Himself said, "I will" step forward and rescue My people. In essence God declared, "You cannot live up to My righteous requirements of obedience; but if you'll trust Me, I'll be your supply."

Where does God take up residence (Ezek. 36:26-27)?

What did God already know about your heart (Jer. 17:9)?
- ○ **it's good**
- ○ **it's deceitful**
- ○ **it's selfish**
- ○ **it's stubborn**

Does this hit you in a new way? When we ask Christ to come into our hearts, He really does. He comes to change us from the inside out. How does this change your theology from seeing God as a duty to a delight?

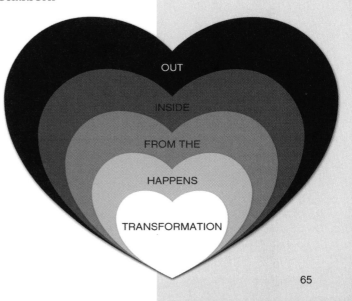

OUT
INSIDE
FROM THE
HAPPENS
TRANSFORMATION

Christ coming to live in our hearts is not cute church jargon. Seeing the absolute depravity of our nature, in His foreknowledge God made a decision to extend an invitation—an invitation He would deliver. Coming to change us from the inside out. Let's remember another place we've heard covenant talk.

What did Jesus specifically call His blood? Why (Matt. 26:26-28)?

Read Jeremiah 32:40-41. What one word describes God's attitude in doing all of this for us?

Sounds a lot like the God of Psalm 145, doesn't it? Perhaps you feel like such a work in progress. Maybe you've done some things, even as a Christian, that you're not proud of. Beloved, God is not looking for perfect people. He's looking for surrendered people. He knew we were messed up from the beginning. Again, our sinfulness never took God by surprise.

The amazing new-covenant promise is that forgiveness and cleansing, restoration and transformation are ours for the taking. All we have to do is call on Christ.

Our desire to love God will never compare with His desire to love us. Our God is passionate about saving the ones He lovingly created. So much so that He does it with every bit of His own heart and soul. Girlfriend, God doesn't just love you. He's crazy-wild about you and cannot wait for you to stop resisting and start resting.

God Is Our Protection, *Always*

When I was a young girl, I longed for someone to come and rescue me. Anytime I saw families that looked halfway functional, the desire to live with them played constantly on my mind. I had a few relatives who were really, really sweet. I always wished I could live with them. Unfortunately, I have no memory of ever feeling truly loved.

Now, please don't feel sorry for me. God has been more than good. I have in-laws I couldn't have handpicked better, and I've gotten to know my birth father. He's the sweetest dad ever. I'm not having a pity party. I'm just stating the facts.

How would you state your facts? How did you feel growing up?

- ○ **loved**
- ○ **secure**
- ○ **rejected**
- ○ **fearful**
- ○ **wanted**
- ○ **like a bother**

How has this shaped your ability to receive love from others?

How do you think it's impacted your ability to receive love from God?

How we're treated in our formative years profoundly affects the way we relate to people today. Many of us neither came to Christ as young children nor were raised by godly, loving parents. Our early experiences make understanding the love of God more difficult. Add the complexities of early neglect, broken trust, and family dysfunctions, and a wounded, handicapped heart can result.

If we have known loving care, then our ability to receive and give love in relationships will be greatly enhanced. For those of us who did not have healthy intimacy in our formative years, the ability to trust can be quite a challenge, especially with God. We're all prone to building invisible protective walls, but those of us who lacked healthy love growing up build castles. For us, trust is a huge issue. This is a lesson I have lived big-time. I was one walled-up girl.

Some years ago a friend paid me a visit. Nothing could've prepared me for a question she'd obviously come to ask. "Tammie, what is it about you that you don't let people close to you? What are you afraid of that you won't let people in? You seem like you are trying to hide something." I was stunned.

Then God began showing me that my visitor was dead-on about me. I *did* have a problem with allowing people into my heart. The problem was not so much that I didn't want to be close to people. I longed for deeper relationships. The problem was I couldn't trust. Anytime my walls would start coming down and I'd find myself becoming vulnerable, my wounded inner carpenter would go into freak mode and start building walls.

What I love about the Lord is that He never uncovers an area without having a gracious plan to do something about it. He does not expose for exposure's sake alone. God's intent for uncovering any areas where we need some help and healing will always be for applying the medicine of who He is to that place.

How would you rate your ability to trust people?

Do you relate with the Lord in any similar ways? If so, how?

I'M TRUSTING

I'M CAUTIOUS

How we associate in our interpersonal relationships definitely spills over into our relationship with the Lord. How can I be so sure of this? Because it all comes from the same heart. We are notorious for projecting what we've sustained in one relationship into another.

I'M SUSPICIOUS

What did God promise to remove from the people (Ezek. 36:26)?

Have you noticed how quickly your inner carpenter builds when your meter of relational danger starts to rise? If so, what do you usually do when you start feeling relational danger?

Do you find yourself making inner promises when you get upset with people? If so, list the kinds of promises you make.

Some of us probably tuck tail and run. We don't like conflict, so we'd rather hide than rock the boat. Others of us are a little more hotheaded. We tend to blow up.

No matter what we do in our protective patterns, most of us make lots of inner promises. If we've been hurt, we make promises such as, "I will never let myself get that close to anyone again." If our trust has been betrayed, we pledge, "I will never let myself need anyone."

Stone by stone we build our walls of protection with all sorts of inner promises. We fail to see that the stone is lifeless, hard, and void of feeling. Our efforts seek to make our hearts the same.

God uncovered in me that I not only had trust issues with people but deep down I also had trust issues with God. Is He really safe, and does He really love me like He says He does? Is He just a control freak who has a really big ego? Or can He really be trusted as a good God?

In the margin read the examples of how we can struggle relationally with God as a direct result of needs not met in earthly relationships; then answer the questions below.

1. If we had an absence of intimacy with an earthly father, we will be inclined to struggle with our Heavenly Father's love for us.

2. If those in authority over us have abused their authority, we will be much more inclined to struggle with God's authority.

3. If we didn't feel accepted and valuable, we will definitely struggle with our worth in God's eyes.

4. If we lived under the hurtfulness of favoritism, we will believe our Heavenly Father plays favorites too.

Can you think of any additional examples? If so, what are they?

Have you struggled with any of the examples? If so, how are you finding victory in allowing God to minister to those areas?

Life can be rough sometimes, can't it? I doubt that any of us can say all of our needs have been met, no matter how well we were parented or how wonderful our relationships were and are. I am so glad God offers us a brand-new heart.

Did you know that in Scripture the heart is identified as the seat of the emotions, personal will, and intellect? The promise of a new heart means every fiber of our being is stamped with the newness of God. God's promise means a deep ministry to the depths of our being—where we think, where we act, and you better believe how we feel.

What happens to those who rely on their own walls (Isa. 30:12-13)?

_____

○ they crash   ○ they get fearful   ○ they get bitter
○ they find satisfaction

Girlfriend, when we rely on our own defenses, we reject God's message of present protection. We have to recognize that our defenses are deceitful to us and will eventually become oppressive for us. An emotional collapse is usually not too far away.

A few years ago I went through a terrible season of hurt in a relationship. It was more than I could take, and I really struggled with isolating myself. I didn't want to be near anyone because I felt so raw around people. I couldn't really hide the pain I was in because my face tells on me so easily. After some time of working it out with the Lord, I felt that His Spirit said to me: *"Tammie, I will hold you together. You don't need to isolate yourself. This will harm you instead of protecting you. Trust Me, Darling."* (And yes, just in case you're wondering, God does talk *darling* talk.)

List the four ingredients for finding daily salvation and strength in the Lord (Isa. 30:15, NIV).

1.   2.   3.   4.

_____   _____   _____   _____

Why do you suspect repentance is mentioned first?

I believe these four ingredients form the pillars of a rich and satisfying relationship with the Lord, beginning with repentance every time. Let me tell you what repentance does for us. Repentance keeps the garden of our hearts clean from any self-protective building supplies; it helps us stay alive and sensitive to the presence of God. Perhaps some of us struggle so much with a lack of confidence before God because the gardens of our hearts stay stony with building materials.

Confidence Booster and Scripture Premise

Can you quote Confidence Booster 3 and Ephesians 1:11 from memory? Try writing them in the margin without peeking. Tell what changes the "inheritance" of God is making in your life.

What did Isaiah say about the heart of God (30:18-19)?

How is this promise like the promise of Hebrews 4:16?

Do you see how great the Father's love is for us?
In His redeeming love, He promises to be our divine rescue. All He requires is that we cry out in repentance and ask for His help.

Promise 4
God Is Our Rock

Have you ever had a mountain-top experience with God only to come tumbling down the mountain afterwards? Yeah, it's not very fun. Not only did I fall down the mountain, I landed in the pit of depression. The problem was I didn't know how to return to everyday living. Couple that with a serious rejection and an enemy who preys on our vulnerabilities and my whole internal world fell apart. No matter how hard I tried, I could not pull myself together.

Some days I thought I'd lose my mind. Fear gripped me like a giant icy fist. As I thought of Job, questions plagued me. "Lord, if You're allowing the enemy to get this close, how much further will You allow?" I was scared out of my mind. Tears were my constant companions, and my friends hardly knew what to do but pray.

One day my dear friend, Shannon, showed up at my door. She had a huge stone in her arms that she was obviously holding with all her might. All my foggy mind can remember her saying was, "God told me to get this for you. I saw it while I was out. It's an old church cornerstone." She didn't stay long before we hugged and said our good-byes.

I was clueless what this meant, so I asked the Lord what I was supposed to do with this. Here is what I heard in my heart as clearly as I'm saying it to you: Lay it beside your bed, and when you wake in the morning, stand on it. This will be a sign to you and your confession that I am your Rock and will hold you together. I will be the wall of protection around your heart.

What is Christ called in Ephesians 2:20?

Beloved, a cornerstone holds the whole building together. God did exactly as He said He would. He held me together, and I found rest in His arms. Perhaps you need your own stone. It doesn't have to be fancy like mine. You may even have one in your yard. A stone can be a reminder of God's faithfulness, or it may be used differently.

What were the Israelites doing in Jeremiah 32:35?

How might the walls we build around our hearts be a form of idolatry?

Much of our self-protecting behavior amounts to idolatry because God is our protector. I'm not talking about the kind of dangerous relationships we need to flee. I mean the interpersonal dysfunction we create by

seeking to protect ourselves by control or passive aggression. In our attempts to protect ourselves, we not only harden our hearts but also wall everyone else out, including the Lord.

Could the invisible barriers you have felt with the Lord be walls that you have built? Perhaps inner promises you've made in times of fear have actually kept your heart desensitized to the Lord and from receiving all that He has for you.

If so, take your pride and barriers to the Lord right now and ask Him to forgive and free you. Pray a prayer of repentance for trying to be your own protection. Then ask the Lord to destroy all those walls.

What two specific requests did the psalmist make in Psalm 86:11?

1.

2.

What did the psalmist expect the results would be if he received his two specific requests?

1.

2.

The response to being taught by the Lord should always be an altered lifestyle that honors God. The psalmist clearly understood this. I love the Amplified Bible's translation of this portion of Scripture.

"Teach me Your way, O Lord, that I may walk and live in Your truth; direct and unite my heart [solely, reverently] to fear and honor Your name" (Ps. 86:11, AMP).

Sometimes a divided heart can appear as innocent as mindless distractions—like roaming around online for hours or watching too much television. I am not saying the Internet or television is bad, but we have a problem when these activities eat too much of our time by taking our focus away from Jesus. When the Holy Spirit starts nudging our hearts toward spending time with the Lord and we choose spiritual laziness by hiding in the distractions of this world, that's when the breakdown in our relationships begin to occur.

"Teach me
Your way, Yahweh, and
I will live by Your truth.
Give me an undivided mind
to fear Your name."

PSALM 86:11

How does a divided heart keep you from honoring the Lord in your daily life?

Distractions like these interfere with our delight in Jesus when we give in to them without discipline. For a while now God has been teaching me to offer Him things that easily distract me and allow Him to put limitations on me. For example, sometimes I limit being online to checking e-mail. I especially love photography and messing with graphics online, but if I spend too much time online, I can start feeling dry with the Lord.

In what ways do you guard your heart from distractions? Give this some thought, and then brainstorm with others in your small group to compile tools you can use to keep your delight in Jesus.

Check what distracts you when you feel spiritually lazy.
○ the telephone
○ everybody else's business
○ shopping too much
○ online social networks
○ television
○ surfing the Internet
○ other: _____
_____
_____

Do you feel like you are winning the battle?
If not, what might you start doing differently?

Can you see how Adam and Eve and the Israelite people struggled with these same challenges?
If so, describe how you think their hearts were divided.

Confidence Booster and Scripture Premise

—

Try writing or reciting these aloud. What key words speak to you? Have you had a chance to share with anyone what you are learning? If so, how?

Read Jeremiah 32:37-39, and paraphrase God's promise to His people.

How does everything about our relationship with the Lord come back to our hearts (v. 39)?

Spiritually speaking, consider how your delight in God would change if you continually allowed Him to gather you ...

in your thought life

in your worries

in your passions

in your longings

The new-covenant promise is that God supplies the singleness of heart to fear His name. This means we neither have to muster up within ourselves the inclination to follow God nor find more spiritual determination. God will do this for us if we follow His leadership. He is pursuing us. We must come out of hiding so we may be caught in His magnificent, heart-arresting, and transforming love.

God Is Our Counselor

God primarily speaks to our hearts from the pages of Scripture and in our prayer times. Most assuredly He speaks at other times as well, but our personal time with Him is foundational. Our insides as believers were crafted for Him when He made us new creations in Christ Jesus.

How did Jesus describe the Holy Spirit in John 14:16,26?

○ **as a Counselor**   ○ **as a Commander**

○ **as a Dictator**   ○ **none of these**

What is the Holy Spirit's specific job description?

In simple terms, the Holy Spirit talks to us about the things of God. Without the consistent spiritual nourishment provided by the Spirit's direction, we will inevitably lose our sense of security before Him. We need a deep understanding of His heart. Healthy confidence blooms from the soil of knowing the heart of God. Only when we feel familiar with God's heart will we feel safe in His presence.

Satan attacks our communication with the Lord because our enemy knows receptivity to God plays a huge role in our security with God. If Satan can cause us to entertain the lies that God is disinterested in us and disappointed with us, he essentially wins because our insecurities keep us disengaged.

What two benefits from Ephesians 1:17 can you start asking God for in order to know Him more?

Accepting anything less than growing intimacy with God is a raw deal. The Holy Spirit brings you wisdom and revelation so you may know God better. Don't settle for less than He intends.

Perhaps you've felt that following hard after God isn't worth it. The call seems too difficult, the payoff so distant. Satan works to promote that idea because he's afraid of what we will be like if we really see God. Remember Satan has seen God with his own eyes. He wanted to be just like Him (Isa. 14:14).

Paul prayed for wisdom and revelation for us (Eph. 1:17). "Wisdom" (*Sophos*) "denotes a fear of God and an understanding of His ways ... It does not necessarily imply brilliance or scholastic training" (Thank You, Jesus!); rather it "indicates the ability to apply skillfully what one knows."[2] "Revelation" (*apokalypsis*) means "to reveal, uncover. ... not merely the thing shown and seen but the interpretation, the unveiling of the same."[3]

When you tie these two words together, revelation offers a fuller disclosure of the Lord while wisdom helps us with the skillful ability to take what we've seen of the Lord and move forward with it.

> "The one who has My commands and keeps them is the one who loves Me. And the one who loves Me will be loved by My Father. I also will love Him and reveal Myself to him."
>
> **JOHN 14:21**

What two things did Jesus promise (John 14:21)?

How do you think the promise corresponds with wisdom and revelation?

How would your obedience change if you viewed it as a way for God to love you more and reveal Himself to you more?

Oh Sister, God never asks us to do something that isn't for our own good. I'm going to stop now and put my face to the floor. Maybe you should too.

God Is Our Inheritance, and We Are His

This past week my husband really lost his cool at the law office. He said, "They probably never want to speak to me again." You see, they were messing with his inheritance.

Did you know Scripture overflows with the subject of inheritance? God wove an earthly and heavenly inheritance from the Book of Genesis to the Book of Revelation. The Israelites themselves were an inheritance for the Lord among all the other peoples of the earth.

> **Read slowly through Ephesians 1:3-19, and look for suggestions of our inheritance. Mark each one in your Bible. Then write a summary statement of what you found.**

Look one more time at the new-covenant promise God made with His people. We want to develop the subject of inheritance and discover how the believers' inheritance plays out in the New Testament.

Read Jeremiah 32:37-41 and Ezekiel 36:24-28, marking every reference to property and land.

What specific land did God promise Abraham (Gen. 17:5,8)?

Now go to Numbers 32:10-13. Which two people did God say would enter the promised land? Why?

In the following verses note what Scripture tells us about Joshua.

Joshua 1:1-3,5

Joshua 8:1-2

Joshua 24:28-30

I love the fact that God eventually called Joshua and the people to fight for their promise. Have you ever noticed how most of us tend to value something much more when we've had to give our all for it? Some fights are worth it. Fighting for victory in Jesus is one of them.

Have you ever had to fight really hard for a victory? If so, what lesson(s) did you learn in the process?

Do you have a current area in your life where you need to fight for a victory? If so, what would it take to move you forward?

I believe the hard-fought lessons where we forge current testimonies for God end up sticking the best. There we find the wisdom and mercy to encourage others. We don't soon forget places we struggled because the hard work of faith leads us to see God's faithfulness.

What did Abraham have that helped him reach the promised land (Heb. 11:8)?
○ determination   ○ resolve   ○ focus   ○ faith

God often used an external work in the lives of the Israelites to demonstrate the internal work of Christ in New Testament believers. One commentator notes, "As the inheritance of the earthly Canaan typified that of the heavenly," we discover that our inheritance is both "future, in the new heavens and earth," and "present, in the here and now."[4]

The Holy Spirit coming to dwell in our hearts through faith has given us a glorious inheritance. Just as the ancients were required to obediently follow the voice of the Lord by faith to attain their earthly promised land, we New Testament believers are also required to obediently follow the voice of the Lord to attain our present, earthly spiritual promised land. He has promised to inspire us toward following Him, but we must mix His inspiration with active faith.

Read 2 Corinthians 1:20-22. Are you actively standing on the promises of God for your life? Girlfriend, this is where you walk in your own land of Canaan.

Have you allowed the enemy to bully you into believing that certain promises of God are not for you? If so, explain.

Would you be willing to let God do a fresh work in those areas of your heart? If so, invite Him into those places to begin transforming how you have believed.

As we pray through our areas of struggle, God's Spirit saturates our inner beings. This is exactly where transformation happens—when it's just you and God working through the deeper issues of your heart. We can easily get in the habit of breezing by and never truly dialoging with God about the real issues of our lives. What we fail to understand is that when we do this, we succumb to shallow Christianity. Deep down we don't want that, right?

Whether you struggle with temptation, weariness, fear, failure, suffering, oppression, or some other issue, you don't have to sink into an emotional hole of isolation, condemnation, guilt, denial, or loneliness. Stand on your fortified foundation of truth. You can always know where you stand with God. You know He bids you come and seize Him. He is your inheritance.

This is when I wish we could sit together over a good cup of coffee. We'd have a sweet conversation about what God is showing you through His Word. I would love to hear all about how you are seeing yourself in light of God's truth and how it is daily changing your approach of Him.

I'd also share that I have to choose daily to believe all these same things. None of us has arrived. Not even our favorite pastors, teachers, or those we deem spiritual giants. All of us direly need our Savior as long as we draw breath.

We have been ingesting a consistent message of the grace of God. He has sought us out for His own inheritance. He has chosen us before the foundation of the world, redeeming us with His own blood and body. He promises us He'll continue to do every bit of work in our hearts if we'll just believe.

You're chosen, covered, and cleansed, my friend—literally from the inside out. Welcome it. Thank Him for it. Embrace it more fully than you ever have before. God handpicked *you* before the foundation of the world.

Receive your spiritual land of promise: You are His, and you are redeemed.

wrapping things up

A FEW LAST QUESTIONS

1. Can you describe in simple terms what *atonement* means?

2. What is the difference between guilt and conviction?

3. When your relational danger meter starts pinging, how will you respond?

4. How is your perception of God changing from duty to delight?

5. How did your Confidence Boosters and Scripture Premises help you this week?

As God Has Promised, Know Your Rights!

1. You can trust in God's faithfulness.
2. You can trust in God's transformation.
3. You can trust in God's protection.
4. You can trust in God's stability.
5. You can trust in God's counsel.
6. You can trust in God's lavish inheritance.

Father, I am in awe of Your redeeming love—that You'd come after me like You have, promising to give me everything I need for intimacy with You. Thank You for never giving up on me and being faithful even when I'm not. You are better than You have to be and more loving than any of us deserve. By the help of Your Spirit within me, bring my whole heart into unity with Yours. Cause my heart to beat for what Your heart beats. I know I can never love You the way You love me, but I want You to know I long to spend my days trying. Do this in me, I pray. In Jesus' mighty name. Amen.

1. Frank Gaebelein, gen. ed., *The Expositor's Bible Commentary*, vol. 6. (Grand Rapids, MI: Zondervan, 1986), 576.

2. Spiro Zodhiates, gen. ed., *Key Word Study Bible* (Chattanooga, TN: AMG Publishers, 1996), 1672.

3. Ibid., 1590.

4. Ibid., 1641.

Going from Duty to Delight

FOURTH STOP

Knowing God Has
Supplied Us

How do we trigger more of the Holy Spirit's power in our lives? We're going to look at several answers to that question. No matter our church backgrounds and differences in theology, we need to learn how to abide daily in His power and activity. Welcome to week 4. Enter a rip-roaring encounter with the Holy Spirit.

How do we trigger more of the Holy Spirit's power?

1. Rely on His leadership.
2. Yield to His pruning.
3. Regularly practice repentance.
4. Inspect your crops often.
5. Set yourself apart.
6. Do not give up.

How
of

Jesus Christ, the glorious Father would give you a spirit of wisdom and revelation in the knowledge of Him. I pray that the perception of your mind may be enlightened so you may know what is the hope of His calling, what are the glorious riches of His inheritance among the saints."

Ephesians 1:17-18

Rely on His Leadership

I am exceedingly proud of you for doing your homework week after week. This praise doesn't come without reason either. I have a handful of incomplete studies sitting on my shelves.

Good intentions and peer pressure assail everyone, don't they? You wouldn't believe how many times I've started a book because it was a friend's new craze or because the pretty cover pulled me in. Then when I didn't finish it, I felt so guilty. Especially when the friend asked whether I was done yet.

Um, well, stutter–stutter. How do you tell someone who was jumping out-of-her-skin excited over a book that you didn't really care for it? It's a sad moment indeed.

You want to hear what I'm learning? I'm learning that God wills and works in me for His good purpose (Phil. 2:13). It goes for you too. Our gung-ho efforts and brainless mistakes happen much less if we'll rely on the Holy Spirit's leadership—even in the minutest of ways. If we'll stay in tune with the Spirit, He will lead us in every way.

DO YOU HAVE A BOOK OR BIBLE STUDY THAT SITS UNFINISHED?

What's its name, how did you aquire it, and why did you lose interest?

Describe a time when you wish you'd relied more on the Holy Spirit's leadership.

Here's mine. A few summers ago I met a woman during our family vacation in Cozumel with *the* most rocking body. We were around the pool, kids playing in the water, and finally when I couldn't stand it any longer I just said it, "Girlfriend, you look good! What in the world are you doing?"

That question opened her floodgates, and she told me Bikram yoga had changed her life. Beyond aerobics, beyond jogging, beyond the treadmill, and even cycling, Bikram yoga was, hands down, what did the trick. When I inquired of yoga's pagan spirituality, she assured me not to

WEEKLY SESSION ANNOUNCEMENTS

Begin familiarizing yourself with Confidence Booster 4 and your Scripture Premise.

Don't let up reciting Confidence Boosters 1, 2, 3, and Ephesians 1:4,7-8,11-12.

Ask God for opportunities to share with someone the truths you are learning.

How's your service opportunity going? Have you served anyone yet?

Have a red marker or pen on hand as you do your homework this week.

worry. She was a believer and solely focused on Christ the whole time. Hmm … I liked her answers.

So guess what I did? I drove 25 miles and paid $25 for a class to get me looking like her. My daughter Peyton even went with me, which actually makes $50 since I paid her way.

I was flat on my back on a nasty floor 95 percent of the time. I was so sick to my stomach in that 100-degree room for 1.5 hours that I thought I was going to die. At one point while I was lying on the floor and Peyton was doing her thing we locked eyes, and I was so overcome with how ridiculous I must've looked—up, down, up, and back down. We almost died laughing. Then we were called out for noise. You better know I felt like a big 'ole case of stupid.

I couldn't get out of there fast enough. Please tell me I didn't *really* just pay $25 (wait, make that $50) and drive 25 miles to lie on a gross, sweat-infested floor to feel hot, nauseated, and ashamed for an hour and a half? Yep. I sure did. That's what happens when I don't submit myself to the Spirit's leading.

continually

most of the time

some of the time

occasionally

How often would you say you look to the Spirit for everyday decisions and living?

Compare Ezekiel 36:26-27 with 1 John 4:13-16 and John 14:16-20. Who is the Spirit?

Signs of the Spirit in Scripture

(If you'd like, jot down any interesting thoughts.)

- **in creation** *(Gen 1:2)*
- **in the exodus** *(Isa. 63:7-10)*
- **in Joshua's life** *(Num. 27:18)*
- **in Ezekiel's life** *(Ezek. 2:1-5)*
- **in Micah's life** *(Micah 3:8)*
- **in the Servant-Messiah's life** *(Isa. 11:2-3; 61:1-3)*

God chose us, redeemed us, and promised us His Spirit. He also came as our sole supply. As my mentor would say, "Want He more praise?" May the rocks not cry out on our behalf. That's all I'm saying.

This progression of intimacy should testify to our hearts. We never have to worry where we stand with God. We are secured for all eternity. We have safety and certainty. Our God is completely healthy and stable. He has no sick need to give love and take it away. He does not paint us a blue sky and turn it to rain without a good and loving reason. Our God will never wake up one day and be over us. Neither do we have to worry which version of Jesus we'll get on any given day. Sister, you'll find no eggshells on the floor around Jesus.

God's heart is yours and mine forever. He is the ultimate promise keeper. This week we want to explore that plentiful supply.

What would your life be like if you fully rested in the fact that God has nothing but good for you?

I'm convinced we'd move to a marvelous place of riding the winds and waves with God if we really came to rest in His love. We'd know spiritual revival to the uttermost. We'd get busy doing the work God has designed for us because we'd be free. Spiritual insecurity would no longer slay us and render us powerless.

Recall the three past Confidence Boosters, and note how they are helping you overcome spiritual insecurity.

1.

2.

3.

RECOMMENDED
READING

Forgotten God
FRANCIS CHAN

Secrets of the Vine
BRUCE WILKINSON

Close this portion by breaking down your Scripture Premise into three parts. Read it in several translations. You can find them for free at *www.mystudybible.com*.

1.

2.

3.

HOW do we trigger more of the Holy Spirit's power?

Yield to His Pruning

Read John 15:1-16.

———

Where does Jesus call us to remain, and how do we stay there (vv. 4,9-10)?

What is Jesus really after in you (v. 11)?

Sometimes we confuse pruning with punishment.

Maturity in Jesus requires grasping the fact that He desires to take us deeper, and He uses the **3 P's of pruning** to take us there: **Pressures, Problems,** and **People**.

Did you know a vinedresser uses specific tools for pruning, and he never cuts without having a goal? He tenderly keeps watch over the grapevine and thins its growth until it reaches maturity. Did you also know that very rocky soil produces the best flavor in the grapes? The farmer even pours gravel into the soil. I recommend Margaret Feinberg's *Scouting the Divine* if you want to explore the work of the vinedresser.

Over the last seven years I've felt that God repeatedly dragged me through the gravel face-first. Life has been ridiculously hard with one situation after another. I'm talking death, depression, rejection, a broken friendship—all coupled with God's call on my life to ministry.

Pouring into others becomes difficult when you're such a broken vessel yourself. Just when I'd reach a point where God was setting me back to my feet and picking the pebbles from my face—back down I'd go. For this former perfectionist, that is very humbling—especially when tears were my closest friends. But you know what? I've come to realize that humbling me was His point the whole time.

How has the Lord used pressures, problems, and people to humble you?

In what ways are you being pruned, possibly that you've not realized until today?

Pruning narrows our focus and strengthens the quality of our fruit. It trains and maintains us by breaking our rebellion, insensitivity, and ever-so-independent spirits. By cutting us back God shapes us into the image of Christ. It keeps us alive and growing in the fellowship of His Spirit.

Pruning weans us from distractions, time wasters, addictions, and selfish habits. It separates us from dead works that God never called us to do or from which He's long since called us. In pruning, the enslaving need for constant affirmation of our flesh is finally hacked. In pruning, God insists on us having more of Him.

Be encouraged, my sister. Jesus never planned for crop failure in your life (John 15:16). Neither should you.

Regularly Practice Repentance

I've waited for weeks to finally arrive at this place with you. We will dive deeply into the topic of repentance. I bet you've wondered when we would. I would have.

First, let me explain my delay. Have you ever met a two-year-old who delights in obeying an authority he or she does not know? If you have, you've encountered a rare find.

We are that suspicious two-year-old. We've not fully visited repentance until today because *have to* obedience and *want to* obedience are worlds apart. One motivates us to analyze self, the other to worship God. Let me give you some examples.

"I know I need to spend time with God, but ...
I know I need to read my Bible, but ...
I know I need to pray more, but ...
I know I need to forgive, but ...
I know I need to love, but ...
I know I need to obey, but ...
I know God loves me, but ..."

"I need to" reflects a duty mentality, where we dread the things of God. Read Romans 7:15–8:2 with the two approaches to obedience in mind.

As Paul determined, Jesus changes our "want to." Deep down we want God, even if we're feeling powerless.

What does the Spirit have that we need, and where we can place our hope (Acts 1:8)?

The basic definition for the *power* of the Holy Spirit means *to be able*.[1] Please take this in: The "to be able" came to live in you and in me. What if we began calling Him the To-Be-Able instead of the Holy Spirit? Can you imagine how that would change our thinking? We'd no longer be ruled by *I can't* because the To-Be-Able can.

This, my friend, is what walking in the Spirit looks like. It's turning to the To-Be-Able all the time. It's also where our "have to" dies and a glorious resurrection of our "want to" rises.

OK, back to repentance. No one has ever said that repentance is easy, but it is worth it.

I've had enough of just feeling bad and being sorry. I want to be free. I want to see the power of God in a mighty way in me. I want to be enraptured by His love.

Sister, this takes turning every bit of who we are over to our To-Be-Able. I'm talking face to the floor, sheer desperation, begging for His forgiveness, and receiving His grace repentance. Not a "God, please forgive me for my sin"—where we cover sin with a blanketed prayer. I'm talking "God, please forgive me for my jealousy and the way I slandered her character."

Repentance isn't "I'm sorry I got caught." It's a "I'm totally undone here. Please, Lord, forgive me, wash me, and make me new."

If you didn't like your answer, it's quite all right. As long as you're willing to work with the Lord on it, I praise you for your honesty. Truly, the closer we walk with Jesus, the more His light will shine on our darkness. Something's amiss if our own depravity apart from Christ isn't ever before us. I'd even venture to say our awareness of our wretchedness needs to grow. Not our wretchedness—our awareness of it. Spiritually speaking, the way up is always down, to our knees, to our faces.

How did the spiritual giant—the apostle Paul—see himself (1 Tim. 1:15)?

How often do you confess your sin to the Lord like this?

- ○ **not enough**
- ○ **every day**
- ○ **every few days**
- ○ **when I feel guilty**

Keeping the subject of repentance before us is not only necessary but also enormously vital. Repentance means giving ourselves a biblically correct spanking and throwing ourselves wholly on the mercy of Christ. Repentance also destroys the Devil's work.

Read 1 John 3:1-9.

_____

In what are we to actively participate (v. 3)?

Why did the Son of God appear (v. 8)?

Do John's words—that those born of God don't sin—seem difficult to understand? Look what the *Key Word Study Bible* says about the passage.

> "John is not teaching the possibility of sinless perfection; he is merely indicating that the person who has experienced regeneration will demonstrate righteousness in daily living. ... Believers are to make the righteousness and holy life of Christ the object of their trust, but also the pattern of their own lives. The expression 'he cannot go on sinning' (v .9) means a true believer cannot sin habitually, deliberately, easily, or maliciously."[2]

Do you have areas where you are "habitually, deliberately, easily, or maliciously" walking in sin? If so, have you confessed this before only to still feel trapped and powerless?

We no longer sin the way the world sins because the Seed of God—the Holy Spirit—lives within us. **Scripture gives us wonderful guidance toward a glorious end of the crazy sin cycle. Want to see it?**

Freedom from the Sin Cycle: 3 Elements to Success

2 CORINTHIANS 7:8-11		ROMANS 8:5-11		HEBREWS 12:4
GENUINE REPENTANCE		**RADICAL RESOLVE**		**RUTHLESS RESISTANCE**
We must beseech the Spirit for genuine sorrow over our sin.		We must beseech the Spirit for holy determination.		We must beseech the Spirit for strong faith muscles.

How are you doing in each of these areas?

Rate your "beseech" quotient for each of the three on a scale of 1 to 10.

What do your evaluations suggest about why you might be stuck in a sin cycle?

When the time of testing comes, in which area do you most need to cry out for the Spirit's help?

Consistent freedom comes when we keep each of these before the Lord in prayer until we see a real harvest of His presence and power. Part of our problem is we repent and find a measure of freedom, but when the time of testing comes, we fall back down. This happens because it takes time to grow a fruitful harvest. We may have experienced a surge of the Spirit's To-Be-Able, but it's not a lasting harvest of freedom yet. We find our harvests when we repeatedly petition the Spirit for Radical Resolve and Ruthless Resistance and then pass some repeated tests.

Perhaps this is exactly what you needed to hear today. Remember me telling you about the focus group that first saw this manuscript? Well, this was a big one for them. Many struggled with cycles of sin and didn't understand why they'd seem to be free, only to end up enslaved again. Galatians 5:1 says, "Christ has liberated us to be free. Stand firm then and don't submit again to a yoke of slavery." Beseeching the Spirit for genuine repentance, radical resolve, and ruthless resistance empowers us to stand firm and free from sin's enslaving yoke.

Inspect Your Crops Often

Now we turn our attention to spiritual harvests. Before we do, let me confess: I know nothing about growing anything. Just ask my friend, Jennifer Hamm. She has long passed me up in preparing, planting, and reaping a harvest from a garden. We've eaten her produce while my seeds collected dust in my shed.

I do, however, know a thing or two about spiritual harvesting. Let's look at some Scripture.

Read Galatians 6:7-10. In your own words describe the message of the text.

Have you seen this law of God at work in your life or in the life of someone you love? How?

With what did Paul equate sowing to please the Spirit (vv. 9-10)?

Now read Galatians 5:16-26. Notice the qualities of the godly or sinful fruit produced by our gardens.

We'll give specific attention to the harvests in our lives using this fruit as our backdrop. We usually cannot see the impact of sin in others, let alone ourselves. We just deal with sin as if we're hoping it will get better. Hear me: Sin never gets better. You can't manage it, wish it away, or pretend it's not there.

Below are suggestions for ways we live to please the sinful nature. Consider this an amplified version of the sinful fruit in Galatians. You can see the connection between seeds and fruit. **When we sow to please our sinful nature, we get these results:**

Slander	Inappropriate language	Lust
False intimacy	Easily angered	Constantly suspicious
Selfish with time	Prone to lying	Addictive practices
Manipulative	Dishonoring of parents	Excusing sin
Habitual negativity	Lack of compassion	Justifying sin
Critical/judgmental	Boastful/arrogant	Seeking false comfort
Secretive with spending	Laziness	Lack of integrity
Sharp with tongue	Controlling	Apathetic with debt
Quick to accuse	Unforgiving	Making fun of people
Prideful	Deceptive intentions	Head games
Impatient	Talking about people	Envy

Read Matthew 15:13. Then have a time of surrender, honest repentance, and Spirit-inspired transformation as you allow God to rip out your sin harvest by its roots.

> "Every plant that My heavenly Father didn't plant will be uprooted."
>
> **MATTHEW 15:13**

Sowing to Please the Spirit

SURRENDER

Walk through each area of your life using the list of sinful fruits as examples of ways you sow to the sinful nature. Dialogue with the Lord, asking Him to shine His loving light on you.

REPENTANCE

Take the appropriate time to repent. Ask Him to give you a godly sorrow over your sin. Ask the Lord to forgive you, cleanse you, clothe you, and restore you.

TRANSFORMATION

Ask the Spirit to rip sin's destructive harvest from your life by the roots (Matt. 15:13).

Sowing to the Sinful Nature in My Own Life

SURRENDER

Lord, how am I sowing to please the sinful nature in my own life?

REPENTANCE

Lord, please forgive me for:

TRANSFORMATION

Lord, please rip out by the roots the sinful harvest of:

Sowing to the Sinful Nature in My Family's Life

SURRENDER

Lord, how am I sowing to the please the sinful nature in my close family relationships (spouse, children, parents, and siblings)?

REPENTANCE

Lord, please forgive me for:

TRANSFORMATION

Lord, please rip out by the roots the sinful harvest of:

Sowing to the Sinful Nature in My Extended Relationships

SURRENDER

Lord, how am I sowing to please the sinful nature in my extended relationships (relatives, friends, church, and work)?

REPENTANCE

Lord, please forgive me for:

TRANSFORMATION

Lord, please rip out by the roots the sinful harvest of:

OK, NOW FOR THE FUN PART.

Go back through each area and ask the Lord to help you identify what godly seed(s) of His Spirit you need to sow with His power.

Get your godly seeds from the fruit in Galatians 5:22-23.

Write the seed of His Spirit boldly over the top of your confessions with your red marker (for Christ's blood), and boldly declare your insistence that the To-Be-Able will come and do it in you.

Confidence Booster and Scripture Premise

Try writing and then reciting your Confidence Boosters and Scriptures aloud.

What key words in the passages are speaking to you now? Has God led you to share with anyone, perhaps a sister who is struggling? If so, who and how?

I am so proud of you. Doing a thorough crop inspection is difficult. I know. This is why I warned you from the beginning that it wasn't going to be easy but it would be worth it. Nevertheless, do not let the Devil steal your gaze from the wonderful work God is doing and has done in you. He loves to upsize our problems and downsize our God. Resist him. Stand firm in the faith.

Blooming with the goodness of Jesus is our goal, and it feels oh-so-good no matter how painful the road to get there. You are well on your way because you've exchanged your sin for repentance. If the Devil tries tripping you up, remind him that you've repented.

Sin resists, but repentance yields.
Sin numbs, but repentance wakes.
Sin separates, but repentance restores.
Sin turns, but repentance faces.
Sin is duty, but repentance is delight.

Set Yourself Apart

Can you think of anything better than staying awed by the Lord?
Today we will hear God say, "You obey Me, and I will stun you with who I am."

What does Hebrews 12:14 tell us to do with holiness?

What will God do if we consecrate ourselves (Josh. 3:5)?

As Joshua spoke of consecration, God called the people to treat themselves as holy. In simple terms: Act like the person I've called you to be.

Scholars call this the two-part process of sanctification: imputed sanctification and pursued sanctification. Imputed sanctification means the holiness that Christ purchased for us. He puts His righteousness in us, giving us brand-new identities (Heb. 10:10). Pursued sanctification means we live up to the truth of those identities by actively working with the Spirit.

Compare Galatians 2:20 and 5:24.
What do the verses have in common?

What will we reap when we live to please God's Spirit (Gal. 6:8)?

According to John 17:3, printed in the margin, what is eternal life?

> "Now this is eternal life: that they may know you, the only true God, and Jesus Christ, whom you have sent."
> **JOHN 17:3, NIV**

Thomas L. Constable defines eternal life as the "life of God that He shares with believers. On the one hand … [it is] a gift that one receives by faith (John 10:28; et. al.). However it also refers to the quality of the believer's life that depends on the extent to which he or she walks with God in fellowship."[3] Holding this thought, now look at John 10:10.

What did Jesus come to give you in abundance?

Constable adds, "Some believers experience eternal life to a greater extent than other believers do."[4]

Are you getting this? If we live lives that please God's Spirit, then He shares more of His life with us. Sounds amazing, doesn't it? This is why we need the To-Be-Able to come and help us. We cannot do obedience alone. We must willingly come to a place where we offer ourselves crucified at His feet—specifically and deliberately.

When we allow God's nature to have free reign, we will experience the life of God. Even though we receive God's Spirit at salvation, we won't reap all the benefits of His power unless we bow low and reside crucified to ourselves.

God told Joshua, "Consecrate yourselves, because the LORD will do wonders among you tomorrow." The Lord will not only do amazing things among us but He will do amazing things in us. Resurrection life doesn't come without death. Power doesn't come without surrender. In the words of Romans 12:1-2, because of God's mercy, we present ourselves as a sacrifice. In response He transforms us.

Perhaps you've already presented yourself as a living sacrifice. Resist the temptation to close your study and call it a day. Spiritual exercises require repetition and greatly sensitize our hearts to the fellowship of the Spirit, keeping us attuned to living in step with His activity.

Personalize the following prayers. Make this prayer time both personal and passionate. Don't rush. Instead, allow the Lord to steal your focus and your heart.

CONSECRATION PRAYER:
PREPARING FOR A WONDER

God, I offer my mind to You today. May every thought, every intention, and every motive be in constant agreement with Your holiness. Please forgive me for every way I have sinned against You with my mind. Please wash my mind and purify it. Empower me to fix my mind on You today. I desire my mind to be set apart for Your glory.

God, I offer my eyes to You today. May everything I choose as entertainment be in agreement with Your holiness. Your Word says in James 4:4 that "friendship with the world is hostility toward God" and "whoever wants to be the world's friend becomes God's enemy." Please forgive me for making friends with the world by not setting my sights on You. Wash my eyes and purify them. Please empower me to fix my eyes on You today. I desire my eyes be set apart for Your glory.

God, I offer You my ears today. May everything I listen to be in agreement with Your holiness. Please forgive me for listening to gossip, slander, and entertainment that builds up the world's ways in me. I also ask for Your forgiveness for not listening to Your Voice in obedience. Please wash my ears and purify them. Empower me to fix my ears on You today. I want my ears set apart for Your glory.

God, I offer my mouth to You today. May every word I speak or do not speak and everything I eat or do not eat reflect Your holiness. Forgive me for every way I have used my mouth as a tool of unrighteousness. Please purify my mouth. Empower me to fix my mouth on You today. Set my mouth apart for Your glory.

God, I offer my heart to You today. May my every feeling, desire, and emotional need come into agreement with Your holiness. Forgive me for seeking fulfillment in temporary satisfactions.

Please wash my heart and purify it. Empower me to fix my heart on You today. I want my heart set apart for Your glory.

God, I offer my hands to You today. May everything I touch or handle show forth Your holiness. Forgive me for using my hands as tools of unrighteousness or withholding service to others. Please wash my hands and purify them. Empower me to fix my hands on You today. I want my hands set apart for Your glory.

God, I offer my feet to You today. May every step I take demonstrate Your holiness. Forgive me for not planting my feet on Your truth and for shrinking back from stepping out with You. Please wash my feet and purify them. Empower me to fix my feet on You today. Please set my feet apart for Your glory.

Confidence Booster and Scripture Premise

———

Try writing your Confidence Boosters and Scripture Premises from memory. Also, take a moment and give God thanks for being all the riches and immeasurable greatness you need.

Do Not Give Up

I love a thunderstorm, especially early in the morning. As long as it doesn't get too out of hand, something about it feels sacred to me.

Yet some storms aren't so sacred—like health-related storms, financial storms, relational storms, or storms of sudden trauma and loss. As we've studied how to live in the power of the Spirit, let's conclude with a critical setback: weariness and discouragement.

Are you or someone you love in a stormy season right now? If so, describe it and explain your foremost concerns.

Refresh your memory with Galatians 6:7-9. What are we encouraged not to do when we get tired (v. 9)?

Do you find this particularly difficult when going through trials?

When does Galatians 6:9 say we will reap a harvest?

Beloved, this is why we need the To-Be-Able more than ever. Unless we have His constant counsel and achieving power running through our brains and veins, we will "become exasperated by difficulty ... be defeated in spirit, discouraged, or faint-hearted."[5]

Sometimes the proper time seems so long in coming, doesn't it? Throwing in the spiritual towel by giving up can be such a temptation for even the strongest among us. Let's face it. Nowhere does the Bible promise us health, wealth, and pain-free living. In fact, the sufferings of Christ flow freely into our lives. If God made His Son perfect through suffering (Heb. 2:10), did we really think we would escape hardships?

Like the apostle Paul, we need to welcome them that we may know Christ and the power of His resurrection (Phil. 3:7-10).

Let me encourage you with what God promised—the presence of Jesus in all our trials. Frankly, if we have Jesus, then we have everything we need. With Jesus we find peace, rest, security, stability, counsel, and profound power to rise above whatever life throws our way.

The Book of Hebrews is quite specific about how God accomplishes holiness in His children.

What tool does He use (Heb. 12:3-13)?
○ **punishment**   ○ **telling off**   ○ **scolding**   ○ **discipline**

Don't get thrown by that word *disciplines*. The word refers to training a child. In biblical times a good father spent much care and patience rearing a son he hoped to make into a worthy heir. F. F. Bruce wrote that "Such a son might have to undergo much more irksome discipline than an illegitimate child for whom no future honor and responsibility was envisaged, and who therefore might be left more or less to please himself."[6] Correction shows we are God's beloved sons and daughters.

Sometimes we just get weary, don't we? The word for "weary" in Hebrews 12:3 intrigues me. It means "fatigued, exhausted, physically or mentally drained."[7] Do you ever feel those things? Taking this kind of weariness into context, read Hebrews 12:1-2 and note what we are told to lay aside and why.

Why do you think Hebrews 12:1 makes a distinction between weights (things that hinder) and sin?

What might be classified as a weight that isn't necessarily a sin?

If you listed things that bring discouragement, frustration, and weariness, I agree. God commended the ancients in Hebrews 11 for their faith. Many of them expressed it through great difficulty. When Hebrews 12:1 says we're surrounded by a cloud of witnesses, might they be cheering you on? Moses or David may be saying, "You can do it, Sister. Don't give up. Keep your eye on the goal. Jesus is so worth it."

Think of a painful time when you saw God's peace and righteousness in the midst of hardship. What did you learn?

I'm tucked away writing in a widow's house. Why in a five-year span she lost her only child and her husband, I do not know. It's been tragic, and I cannot wrap my mind around it. But I can tell you the beauty of the presence of God glows from her face. In the midst of her tragedy I've seen God's peace and righteousness radiate from her life. Excruciating heartbreak has taught her to dwell with Jesus like never before. I admire her greatly. When I look into her eyes, I am looking in the face of a woman living my worst nightmare. Yet she teaches me how God sustains. He's faithful to His children. He really can see us through.

Please read Psalm 62:8 aloud as a prayer.

_____

Now read Isaiah 40:29-31 aloud as a promise.

_____

Hang on and keep looking to the To-Be-Able as your powerful supply. Remember that the Devil wants to upsize our problems and downsize our God. Keep pressing your face to the floor. Crying out in desperation. Laying your whole self before Him. You will see your God. Be a woman of holy determination, accountable for your sin, and pursue a holy life. Perhaps nothing lights a fire in our souls for more of God like seeing a lifestyle of repentance, pruning, consecration, and choosing not to give up or give in.

This, dear one, is how we walk in a greater power of the Spirit and dance in delight.

* **Allot some time before stepping into week 5** to read and ponder Ephesians 1:3-23. Given our progression of study, take the time to connect its message and application with God having chosen us, redeemed us, promised us Himself, and supplied us with His power. Read the passage in *The Message*.

wrapping things up

A FEW LAST QUESTIONS

1. Can you describe in simple terms what *walking in the Spirit* means?

2. What is the difference between a duty mentality and a delight mentality?

3. From now on when your flesh and the Devil say, "You can't," what will you say?

4. How has your perception of God changed from duty to delight?

5. How did your Confidence Boosters and Scripture Premises help you this week?

As God empowers you, know your rights and rest in the fact that ...

1. In every situation the To-Be-Able is your ever-present help.
2. All-out surrender is your friend, not your foe.
3. Transformation is the Spirit's job, not yours.
4. Crop failure is not your lot.
5. Delight is yours, seize it.

Father, I am stunned by Your love and tender mercy. Thank You for being everything I need and more. Forgive me for every way I've not trusted in Your tender care and refused to yield to what You desire to do in my life. Thank You for never letting me go—even forcing obedience for my own good. Help me never to forget the truth that You are my To-Be-Able every time my heart is drawn back to "I can't." You are my Grand Rescue, and I love You so much. In Jesus' powerful and mighty name I pray. Amen.

1. Spiro Zodhiates, gen. ed., *Key Word Study Bible* (Chattanooga, TN: AMG Publishers, 1996), 1612.

2. Ibid., 1439.

3. Thomas L. Constable, *Notes on Galatians* (Sonic Light, 2010), 69.

4. Ibid.

5. Zodhiates, 1613.

6. F. F. Bruce, "The Epistle to the Hebrews" in *The New International Commentary on the New Testament* (Grand Rapids, MI: William B. Eerdmans Publishing Company, 1964), 343.

7. Zodhiates, 1637.

FIFTH STOP

Knowing God Has
Commanded Us

One of the greatest paradoxes of the human soul is love. We soar to highest heights with it and plummet to lowest lows without it. We crave it. We want it. We hate it. We fear it.

God has commanded us to love Him. What do we do with this crazy thing called love? Enter week 5 and see.

To Love God
Forms the Beginning and End of Our Worship

I have wonderful news for you today. The moment you were born again you were born into the greatest love relationship ever known—the love between the Father and the Son.

I once shared this while speaking to a group of women. Instantly tears sprang to many of their eyes. Not only is it the most beautiful thought ever, but it is also something many of us need to hear.

WEEKLY SESSION ANNOUNCEMENTS

Begin familiarizing yourself with Confidence Booster 5 and your Scripture Premise.

———

Don't let up reciting Confidence Boosters 1-4, and Ephesians 1:4,7-8,11-12,17-18.

———

Keep asking God for opportunities to share the truths you are learning.

———

How's your service opportunity going? Have you served anyone yet?

———

Our first three points for this session focus on loving God. The final two focus on loving people.

———

Read John 17:24-26, and relish your inheritance.

Did you know God used the word *love* in Scripture more than the words *obey* and *obedience*? A word search in my Bible software pulled up the numbers. In the *Holman Christian Standard Bible* the word *love* appears 695 times. The word *obey* appears only 183 times and *obedience* 27.[1]

The apostle Paul mentioned and suggested love in another place. See the margin instruction.

Read Ephesians 1:3-23. Highlight every occurrence of the word "love" or any form of it.

How has each week of our study related to love thus far?

Week 1:

Week 2:

Week 3:

Week 4:

Which facet of God's love has spoken to your heart most? Why?

What did Jesus say about love in Mark 12:28-31? How important is it?

Jesus took the whole law and condensed it into one sizable bite: love. He also answered the man with the traditional Jewish "statement of faith," the *Shema*, found in Deuteronomy 6:4. Pious Jews recited those words every morning and evening, as well as Leviticus 19:18.

Many Bible scholars believe the scribe asked sincerely. Unlike most of the men in his religious circle who were hostile toward the Messiah, this man likely desired an honest answer.

The Jewish law contains 613 commandments. Religious leaders hotly debated which commands were most or least important. Because of this, they broke the laws into "heavy and light," hoping to differentiate. In an effort to make the laws doable, they essentially "cluttered up their faith with hundreds of rules derived from traditional interpretations of biblical laws."[2] I'm just speculating, but perhaps the scribe who came to Jesus was worn out from all the performing. Have you ever tried to keep 613-plus laws for a 12-hour period?

Let's explore for a minute some rules we try to live by. Why do we do it, and what happens when we succeed or fail?

To get you thinking I will provide one of my own. Then list some of your rules.

RULES I LIVE BY	WHY?	IF I SUCCEED, I ...	IF I FALL SHORT, I ...
Never be late	Sign of selfishness	Feel accomplished	Feel very anxious

In Mark 12:33 love was particularly more important than what?

Jesus demands an unconditional decision to love God alone far above religious rituals of confession and penance. A commentator explains that such love "determines the whole disposition of one's life and places one's whole personality in the service of God."[3] It "reflects a commitment to God which springs from divine sonship."[4]

Brother Lawrence wrote, "Many do not advance in Christian progress because they stick in penances and particular exercises while neglecting the love of God, which must be the end purpose of all actions."[5]

As a young wife and mom I had a whole lot of rules for living. The only way I thought I would even remotely succeed was to put major boundaries on myself. I would never spank. Never fight in front of my children. Never smoke in the house. Never, never, never …

I carried that same kind of thinking into my relationship with God. I would never miss a quiet time. Never admit to weakness and only have faith. Never, never, never …

Only thing was, my nevers weren't working. I couldn't seem to do everything so perfectly—especially that quiet time thing. One time while sitting in the counselor's chair I confessed my frustration. Her response was shocking:

"Tammie, I think it's time you quit having your quiet time."

What? Had she lost her mind? For a moment I questioned her theology. It felt like she was telling me to walk away from God. The only reason I took her advice was because she had been right about so many other things.

My counselor was dead-on in her advice. As I let go of the "dread" of having to meet with God, suddenly I found myself having a quiet time. God began to replace the dread with a burning flame of desire. With newfound passion I was praying like never before, studying Scripture like never before, worshiping like never before, carrying my Bible to bed and staying awake for hours like never before …

You want to know what really happened?
God set my entire life (heart, soul, mind, strength) ablaze with His love.

With some counterintuitive advice, my counselor led me to a radical discovery. Rightly used, spiritual disciplines form a means to a glorious end. They run us right smack into the love of God. It's great to be trained in the things of God when the disciplines are not rules but vehicles for authentic worship.

Have you been approaching discipline with a rules mentality? Perhaps that chair you've been in for years needs to be replaced with your face to the floor or a walk outside with Jesus. What about trying a new Bible in a new translation or a new worship CD for a new season?

What areas of dread do you need to exchange for a burning flame of love?

The greatest disaster to our faith is making Christianity about rules instead of relationship.

To Love God
Is to Trust His Leadership in All Our Living

Not long ago I was running late for church. I couldn't find anything to wear. Wait, that's not true. I couldn't find anything I *wanted* to wear. Then I did what all good Christian wives and mothers do: I fussed at my family and blamed them for my mood.

Over lunch one of my friends suggested I decide on Saturday night what I'm going to wear the next day. Brilliant! Why didn't I think of that? The only drawback is a night of sleep can change a girl's mind. Cute on Saturday might not be so cute on Sunday. Nevertheless, I took her advice. Only I asked the Lord if He'd be so kind to help as well. Guess what? He did! In no time I had Sunday's outfit ready to go. It was cute. I'd never thought of it before. And I felt skinny in it! Now, before you throw your Bible study at me, hear me out.

We've been commanded to love God with the entirety of our person (heart, soul, mind, strength). Maybe that means God invites us to include Him in everything. What if the command is much broader than simply us having biblically correct thoughts? What if He's inviting us to a place where our whole lives are lived in communion with Him, even in the measliest things, like standing in our closets trying to prepare for the day?

113

What was Adam told to do in the garden (Gen. 2:15-16)?

How about that? He was to eat, work, and obey. Sounds pretty measly, don't you think?

What does Proverbs 16:3 say about including the Lord in our planning?

God desires that we commit to Him whatever we do, and I believe that's going to take God filling us with the knowledge of His will in whatever we do. Proverbs isn't giving permission for blessing as long as we include God in all things. It's describing a bent of the soul toward God in utter receptivity. When we live in that spot, we experience His blessing.

Does something on your heart need God's assistance?
If so, tell Him about it verbally or by writing a prayer below.

Coming to a place of security with the Lord happens when we start trusting His leadership in all our living. God created us for utmost dependence. One way we find confidence in the Lord is when we start taking His hand for help and filtering whatever we do through His presence in our lives.

In Proverbs 16:3 the root of the word *commit* in Hebrew means *to roll,* as in to roll something over to Him. Could loving God with our entire person really look like a life where we roll everything—all decisions, all relationships, all mundane and ordinary living activities—over *to* Him and *with* Him?

For instance, what if we asked the Lord to order our footsteps on a daily basis instead of coming up with our own plans? What if we began asking Him, "Lord, am I to do this or go there?" Can you imagine the frustration we would save ourselves if we checked with God first? After all, He does know all things.

I encourage you to take an inventory now.

How would each of these areas change if you filtered them through the Lord first?

your calendar:

your hobbies:

your finances:

your social media:

Confidence Booster and Scripture Premise

Close this portion by writing your Confidence Booster and Scripture Premise in the margin. Do any key words speak to you? If so, which one(s)?

Have you asked God to anoint you to speak these truths into someone's life?

To Love God
Is to Worship Him in Spirit and in Truth

I want to ask you a question I just asked Savannah, my youngest, and her friend.

What do you think of when you hear the word *balance*?

Would you like to hear their response?

Savannah: Being perfect in all areas but never able to maintain it.

Sarah: Balance takes a lot of work.

Me: Yeah, you have to work to get it and work to keep it, huh?

Them: Seriously.

Turn now to Jesus and a woman at a well. Read John 4:7-26. Let's consider spiritual balance.

What is this balance (vv. 23-24)?

If you had to describe it, what would you say this balance looks like?

In very simple terms, if we lean on too much spirit, we are in jeopardy of developing a faith based on emotions and experiences. If we lean too much toward truth, we are in danger of legalism—the habit of being all about religion and no relationship. Worship in spirit and truth keeps us sensitive to the Spirit and keeps us balanced.

How well would you say you balance spirit and truth?

Is encountering God through prayer and Scripture rich and meaningful to you?

Would you like to know what I do to have a rich and meaningful time with Jesus? I don't offer my process as a cookie cutter recipe. But if you've struggled in knowing how to balance your life with prayer and God's Word, I'd love to share my own Jesus time with you.

Before we walk through this together, here are a couple of things you need to know.

I do not consider this a study time.

I always have a pen and paper.

SIX STEPS TOWARD AN EFFECTIVE JESUS TIME

Submit
Process
Yield
Read
Dialogue
Fill

Step 1: Submit

Openly confess your submission to the Lord's authority. Tell Jesus how much you love Him, desire to worship Him, and how you'd like to love and worship Him more.

Step 2: Process

Tell Jesus what's in the forefront of your mind. Share your fears, insecurities, offenses, health-related concerns, sources of anger, and frustration. Discuss it all. Hold nothing back. Work through repentance of sin. Place decisions before the Lord, asking specific questions and requesting deliberate confirmation. Pray for loved ones and those on your heart.

Step 3: Yield

Offer each part of your body to the Lord through intentional consecration.

Step 4: Read (For today read 2 Pet. 1:3-11.)

Open your Bible to 2 Peter 1:3-11, and ask God to speak to you. Meditate and marinate on the words, phrases, and sentences that capture your attention.

Step 5: Dialogue

Write down those specific promptings. What is God showing you? How is He convicting you? What is He prodding your heart to believe and receive? Should you memorize that verse? Interact with the Word of God with Jesus. Freely ask questions and share doubts.

Step 6: Fill

Ask the Spirit to give you everything you need. Request His To-Be-Able power so you can walk solely in His ways. Seek His heart so you will love Him more than anyone or anything else. Appeal for His equipping so you can walk in perseverance through whatever challenges and trials you face. Desire His love so you can love people with the heart and willingness of a servant. Girlfriend, that is spirit and truth in action. It leads to deep-end swimming with God.

Swim here often—hopefully every day—and it will utterly change your entire life.

To Love God
Is to Choose to Love People

When my girls were young, someone advised me to let them work out their own struggles. How on earth would they ever develop the tools for healthy relationships if I never let them practice? I not only wanted to teach them to relate by ditching their selfishness. I also wanted to teach them how to best love one another.

God enforces the same requirements with you and me. We must love others through practice.

> **Please reread Mark 12:28-31. Did the man ask**
> **Jesus a singular or plural question?**
> ○ singular ○ plural
>
> **What kind of answer did Jesus give Him?**
> ○ singular ○ plural
>
> **Why do you think Jesus gave a two-part answer?**

The man asked Jesus a singular question, and Jesus gave him a plural answer. Why? If you wrote something to the effect that you "cannot have one without the other," you are most certainly right. Perhaps because the love of God is most perfected in us when it's reproduced through us and among us.

We weren't created for aloneness but for relationships. David Ferguson, author of *The Commandment Principle* reminds us: "In Genesis 2:18, God utters these words: 'It is not good.' "[6] When God "declares something to be 'not good,' you have a crisis—a very big deal. So what could possibly be 'not good' about the Garden of Eden?"[7] It was not good for man to be alone.

Why is this a very big deal? Because we are ministers of each other's aloneness. We cannot biblically say, "All I need is God" because we were created to need both God and people. Drs. Henry Cloud and John Townsend point out: "Our deepest need is to belong, to be in relationship, to have a spiritual and emotional 'home.' The very nature of God is to be in relationship: 'God is love,' says 1 John 4:16. Love means relationship—the caring, committed connection of one individual to another. Like God, our central need is to be connected."[8]

Not only have we been born from the greatest relationship ever known but we also are responsible for mirroring the beautiful relationship between the Father and Jesus in all other relationships. **The Great Commandment is one of the fullest expressions of what it means to truly walk in the presence of God.**

How do you see this truth expressed in John 17:20-23?

John 17:23 reflects Mark 12:31. God loves our neighbors, so we are to love them. They will know God loves them when they see us loving both Him and them. When you're at the office, your nearest co-worker is your neighbor. Your little one across the room is your neighbor. Your husband, lying in the bed next to you, is your neighbor. Your mother-in-law, on the other end of the phone, well, you get the point.

How does this change your thinking about loving the people in your life? Would you say you're doing a very good job?

A friend once said, "Most of the time we barrel through life and people become landscape in our peripheral vision." Could the Lord be saying, "How about spending as much time focusing on others as you spend on yourself?"

Confidence Booster and Scripture Premise

How are you doing on these? Try writing them in the margin without peeking.

The *Key Word Study Bible* defines the kind of love Jesus spoke about as "a love rooted in the mind and will of the subject and means to value, esteem, prize, treat as precious … which is done for the benefit of the subject. Theologically, it represents God's action in sending His only Son to die for the world."[9]

To love God and have hearts that beat with His nature means to treat people as having worth. We become a holy reproduction of the love of God that we have received. Definitely not just pretty feelings, love is a choice to honor God—by honoring people. With love we don't treat people as landscape; we treat them as precious gifts.

Do you take time to notice the people in your areas of activity and to treat them with respect? Would their answers be the same as yours?

Beloved, we quench the Spirit quickly when we mistreat and dishonor people. When we treat people as beneath us, we set ourselves up for a holy humbling. Waiters, waitresses, cashiers, and techs all deserve honor and respect. As do our co-workers for whom we may not have an affinity or the postal worker who is obviously having a bad day and doesn't seem to like her job.

Here's some really good news: Did you know this kind of love has an attachment of joy to it? The Greek definition clearly states that loving not only indicates "a direction of the will" but also consists of "finding one's joy in something or someone."[10]

Perhaps the joy we feel is the holy nod of God saying, "Good job. I am proud of you," especially when we love those who are difficult to love.

Have you encountered someone difficult to love? In what ways could you love that person the way God requires?

When the focus group and I came to this section, codependency became a hot topic in our discussion. Many members shared failed friendships because of the toxicity of neediness in their relationships. Some were even struggling with codependency with their mothers—and their mothers were the needy ones.

Some relationships are safe, some are not—even within our own families. In some relationships we cannot win no matter how hard we try or what we do perfectly. Some people constantly pull the rug from beneath our feet through hidden or overt messages. Please hear me:

Loving **does not mean** we dismiss healthy, appropriate boundaries.
Loving **does not mean** being walked on.
Loving **does not mean** going deep with all people.
Loving people **does not mean** never saying no to people.
Loving people **does not mean** we always have to answer the phone.
Loving people **does not mean** we take abuse.
Loving people **does not mean** we let people control us.

At times, the best approach to biblical love is to step back and put a stop to an approval addiction. Sometimes what we're calling love isn't love at all; it's an unhealthy addiction.

The Lord designed us for relationship, but we must guard our hearts from inordinate neediness—people needing us too much or vice versa.

My mentor once pulled me aside for a needed conversation. She was detecting a potential relational danger with a new person in my life:

"Tammie, I need to share something with you. You will love this person best if you love her from a safe distance."

My mentor warned me that areas in this woman's life were potentially dangerous mixed with mine. It's been a while since I received that advice. Long enough for me to watch from a safe distance and to see why her advice was right. This person is still a neighbor in my life, but caution has been my friend. Am I kind to her? Yes. Am I gracious with her? Yes. Am I lovingly guarded around her? Yes. Yes. Yes.

**How might my mentor's advice apply
to one of your relationships?**

Boundaries in relationships are good. We can give so much of ourselves in relationships that we have nothing left for the Lord. Only God

Do you "need" someone too much? If so, lay that relational idol down.

What do you do when you are under duress? Is your first instinct to pick up the phone or to cry out to the Lord?

should occupy the throne of our hearts. We must love without putting our neighbor in the place of an idol. If we continually turn to a person as our help instead of turning to the Lord, we need to stop and test our feelings. We may have built an idol that needs to come down. If we find our minds constantly entertained with another person who isn't close family, a godly romantic relationship, or in the middle of a pressing need or crisis, maybe that person needs to come off that pedestal.

I'm certainly not suggesting we never pick up the phone. I am suggesting we get healthy in our relationships and not give them more weight than they deserve. No human should ever be the center of our universe. That place is reserved only for Jesus.

To Love People
Requires God-given Heavenly Skill

If you and I are going to love our neighbors with any vestige of victory, we need some serious wisdom. After all, some of our neighbors totally wear us out.

One darling young woman never knows where she stands with her boyfriend's family. Sometimes they like her, and sometimes they don't. Another struggles to figure out the women in her singles' group who are sweet as sugar then as cold as ice. Still another wishes her whole extended family would just go away. **What about you?**

- **Are you involved in any hot and cold relationships?**
- **Are any family members driving you nuts?**
- **Are relational circles at your church a challenge?**

In what relationship do you most need wisdom? Why?

Today we take the command Jesus gave to "love our neighbors" and zoom the lens specifically to the wisdom He gives to love people well.

Why do you think the apostle Paul prayed for the Philippians to have "knowledge" and "every kind of discernment" (Phil. 1:9-10)?

When Paul linked "knowledge" with "every kind of discernment," he was describing the "ability to recognize concepts, detect meanings and ideas; to make moral judgments and discriminate between right and wrong, good and bad, wise and foolish."[11]

Has God ever clearly made you an "expert" in a relationship by showing you how to handle the situation in a way you wouldn't have ordinarily known? Describe the situation.

How might that past expereince prompt you to take current relational challenges to the Lord?

God can make us experts in some of our most challenging relationships if we are willing to seek His face and pray. Sometimes He'll even show us that we are the challenging person.

How are we to love according to Romans 12:9?

Some translations say we are to love genuinely or without hypocrisy. All of these are wonderful and correct, but I prefer the NIV: "Love must be sincere." What's more, I totally dig the Greek meaning of sincerity: "inexperienced in the art of acting."[12]

Has the Lord ever rebuked you for superficial sweetness? He has me.

Confidence Booster and Scripture Premise

Quote your Confidence Booster and Scripture Premise from memory. Also, take a moment and give God thanks for being all the riches and immeasurable greatness you need.

INTERESTING FACT: Did you know the Book of Ephesians begins with love (1:4-6) and ends with love (6:23-24)? With what other words does it begin and end?

**Would you say you're sometimes a "love poser?" In
what relationship do you most gravitate to this? Why?**

Sincere love means making sure we're free from being love posers.
Love posers put up with people by faking niceness. It's the opposite of
kindness. Kindness is treating people with dignity and respect out of the
goodness of God's heart within you.

So, how do we break a "love poser" cycle? We own up to our struggle
in prayer and ask the Lord for wisdom. Remember, my friend, the Spirit
is our glorious To-Be-Able.

Have you wished you had better relationship skills? Did you know
another rendering for "wisdom" is "heavenly skill"? Yep. It's in the
Greek. For the last few moments of our session, let's go to a place in
Scripture where God provides a blueprint for the relational heavenly skill
we so desperately need. **Take a minute to read James 3:13-18.**

**What two traits are earthly, unspiritual,
and demonic (vv. 14-16)?**

**Describe a time when you were hurt by
someone's envy and selfish ambition.**

**Is your envy of someone or perhaps your
selfish ambition hurting another person?**

I've felt a great deal of pain over another woman's jealousy and selfish
ambition. How do I know to label her behavior? Because for no apparent
reason she has lied about me, attempted to destroy some of my closest
friendships, and blatantly ignored me when we were in close quarters. It's
been an ongoing situation for several years now, with no solution in sight.

I've done all I can do to love this person. I've tried to talk to her. I've asked her forgiveness if I've hurt her. I've gotten on my face praying for her, and I've sobbed my eyes out over the profound hurt I've sustained because of her.

Sometimes we can do all that's humanly possible to no avail. We just have to hang it up to, "Lord, You know." Ultimately we're not responsible for others' hearts, only our own.

Being women of relational success means we empty ourselves of ourselves. **We have to filter every fiber of who we are through the seven relational "heavenly skills" found in James 3:17**. Take a moment to read the Amplified Version in the margin.

> "The wisdom from above is first of all pure (undefiled); then it is peace-loving, courteous (considerate, gentle). [It is willing to] yield to reason, full of compassion and good fruits; it is wholehearted and straightforward, impartial and unfeigned (free from doubts, wavering, and insincerity)."
>
> **JAMES 3:17, AMP**

Which one speaks to you most?

Which stings you the most?

I picture us as jars filled with dirty water (the sinful nature). If you take our jars (us) and just pour us into another jar (people) without a filter (the Holy Spirit), then you have jealousy, selfish ambition, sinfulness, competitiveness, harshness and insistence on our own rights, obstinance, unyielding spirits, judgment, favoritism, hypocrisy, and pretending.

But if we turn to the Lord, seeking His heavenly skill and relational filtering, what will pour forth from our lives will be pure, peace-loving, gentle, compliant, full of mercy and good fruit, impartial, and sincere.

We let our resentments go. Our anger go. Our frustrations go. Our high expectations go. Our anxiousness and restlessness go. God brings inner transformation as we trust Him. He assures us, "Love your neighbor as yourself, and I'll handle the rest."

Think back to the first question in this segment. I asked in what relationship you need the most wisdom. In that relationship, which of the seven heavenly skills do you need to walk in more?

Loving our neighbor means we choose to do something again and again. What is it, and why (Eph. 4:32)?

Sounds like a big one to swallow, doesn't it? Believe me, I know. How do you forgive someone who has ...

    wronged you? The Spirit's power

    abused you? The Spirit's power

    maligned your character? The Spirit's power

    lied to you? The Spirit's power

    judged you? The Spirit's power

    stolen from you? The Spirit's power.

Why do we forgive? Because we rely on the overflowing power of Jesus Christ.

Forgiveness does not mean jumping back into close relationships with total trust. Forgiveness means we are free from the cage of our own wounds and pain. Forgiveness means we don't rot away with seething anger and resentment. Forgiveness means we trust the heart of our God.

A few years ago, God orchestrated a moment when I came face to face with someone and wholeheartedly forgave. It was huge. The person was my maternal grandmother. I had not spoken to her since I was 15 years old. My grandfather (who's dead now) had sexually abused me, and my grandmother had allowed it. Not just once, but repeatedly.

A few years after our "forgiveness" encounter she lay dying in another state and begged to call and speak with me. Her daughter dialed my number, spoke to me for a moment, and then held the phone to my grandmother's ear. Obviously my prior confession of forgiveness was not enough for her as her life hung in the balance. I will never forget the conversation.

> *Her:* "Tammie, I'm so sorry. I'm so sorry. I'm so sorry. I'm so sorry." (By now, we're both crying.)
> *Me:* "Grandma, I forgive you. I promise you I meant what I said on that driveway that day. You're forgiven. I promise. Grandma, do you know Jesus?"
> *Her:* "Yes. I know Him. Yes. I know Him."

Me: "If you know Jesus like you say you do, when you close your eyes here on earth and open them in heaven, you will open them to see the most beautiful smiling face of Jesus. It will all be over. No more pain. No more guilt. No more fear. No more sin. I totally forgive you, and He does too. Please don't feel guilty anymore."

As I hung up the phone sobbing, you know what pained me most? That she carried that enslaving guilt for two years, even after we had already spoken and reconciled. How can I be so broken for her pain after our history? It's a Spirit work by the Spirit's power.

I never set out to have compassion and mercy. I set out to obey my God who commands me to love Him with all of my heart, all of my soul, all of my mind, and all of my strength, and to love people the way I love myself. If God had not demanded mercy, I never would have given it.

Jesus' leadership alone transformed me from the inside out and gave me the grace to forgive. Watching Him love the people who rejected Him, betrayed Him, spat on Him, and crucified Him spurred me to forgiveness. This was a full-blown Jesus work through and through. It happened through meeting with Jesus, consistently pouring out my heart in spirit and truth, and allowing the Scripture to wash my heart and my mind entirely.

I love what A. W. Tozer said in *The Pursuit of God*: Prying into the mysteries of election, predestination and the divine sovereignty "may make theologians, but it will never make saints."[13] Can I tell you what makes us saints? **Agape: actively inhaling and exhaling the love of God that is found in Christ Jesus.**

Relationships are difficult. No two ways about it. They require the Spirit's power—and hear me now—they are meant to require it. When, and only when, the To-Be-Able of the new covenant supplies us will we do that which we know we could never do on our own.

Perhaps, like me, it's time you finally forgive. God never commands anything of us that He is not willing to supply us with the power to fulfill. Get down on your face and pour your heart out to Him now. He's chosen you. He's redeemed you. He's promised you Himself. He's supplied you with His power.

Sister, "You can do this thing!"

wrapping things up

A FEW LAST QUESTIONS

1. Can you describe in simple terms what the Great Commandment means?

2. What is the difference between biblical love and earthly love?

3. Have you considered memorizing the seven heavenly skills of relational wisdom?

4. How is your perception of God changing from duty to delight?

5. How did your Confidence Boosters and Scripture Premises help you this week?

As God's Commanded, Know Your Rights!

1. You can do this thing!
2. You can do this thing!
3. You can do this thing!

1. Available from the Internet: *http://www.biblegateway.com*

2. Lawrence O. Richards, *The Teacher's Commentary* (Wheaton, IL: Victor Books, 1987).

3. William L. Lane, "The Gospel of Mark" in *The New International Commentary on the New Testament* (Grand Rapids, MI: William B. Eerdmans Publishing Company, 2002), 433.

4. Ibid.

5. Brother Lawrence, *The Practice of the Presence of God* (revised and rewritten by Harold J. Chadwick) (Gainesville, FL: Bridge-Logos Publishers, 1999), 53.

6. David Ferguson, *The Great Commandment Principle* (Carol Stream, IL: Tyndale House Publishers, 1998), 19.

7. Ibid.

8. Dr. Henry Cloud and Dr. John Townsend, *Boundaries* (Grand Rapids, MI: Zondervan, 1992), 64.

9. Spiro Zodhiates, gen. ed., *Key Word Study Bible* (Chattanooga, TN: AMG Publishers, 1996), 1571.

10. Spiros Zodhiates, *The Complete Word Study Dictionary* (Chattanooga, TN: AMG Publishers, 1993), 64.

11. Zodhiates, *Key Word Study Bible*, 1625.

12. Ibid., 1588.

13. A. W. Tozer, *The Pursuit of God* (Camp Hill, PA: Wing Spread Publishers, 1982), 64.

....

Father, I am fully dependent on Your power, and there is nowhere else I'd rather be. I know full well I cannot live this life without You, let alone live up to Your commandment of love. I bring all of me before You and ask You to come and do this relationship thing in me. I know You will, and for this, I am exceedingly grateful. I love You so much, Lord Jesus. Amen and amen.

....

Going from Duty to Delight

SIXTH STOP

Knowing God Has
Secured Our
Victory

**Wishing for victorious living is over.
It's yours, my friend.** Here's the secret:

Keeping the delight you've worked so hard to attain
requires you seize it and stand firm.

Four Requirements to Living Victoriously

1. **Know the Battle That's Raging**
2. **Know the Role Your Identity Plays**
3. **Recognize and Resist Satan's Attacks**
4. **Stand Firm in the Armor of God**
   - **In Truth, Righteousness, and Peace**
   - **In Faith, Salvation, and with a Sword**
   - **In Spirit-Led Prayer**

I Am Victorious

Scripture Premise:

"For He chose us in Him, before the foundation of the world, to be holy and blameless in His sight."

Ephesians 1:4

"We have redemption in Him through His blood, the forgiveness of our trespasses, according to the riches of His grace that He lavished on us with all wisdom and understanding."

Ephesians 1:7-8

"We have also received an inheritance in Him, predestined according to the purpose of the One who works out everything in agreement with the decision of His will, so that we who had already put our hope in the Messiah might bring praise to His glory."

Ephesians 1:11-12

"I pray that the God of our Lord Jesus Christ, the glorious Father, would give you a spirit of wisdom and revelation in the knowledge of Him. I pray that the perception of your mind may be enlightened so you may know what is the hope of His calling, what are the glorious riches of His inheritance among the saints."

Ephesians 1:17-18

"And what is the immeasurable greatness of His power to us who believe, according to the working of His vast strength."

Ephesians 1:19

Requirement 1
Know the Battle That's Raging

I've carried you so long in my heart that I'm struggling with the idea of letting you go. Now instead of writing, I've busied myself with timewasters to deflect my emotions. Long before you decided to study this material I was dying to share it with you. The only way I have relief in cutting you loose is the hope that I'm bidding farewell to a much more secure woman in Christ.

Sister, what in this study has most impacted you?

In this last session I want us to consider how to keep the delight we've worked so hard to achieve. We'll find the answers within the closing words of the same book as our Confidence Boosters and Scripture Premises—Ephesians 6.

Please read Ephesians 6:10-18.

Paul didn't seek to convince his readers a battle was raging. He insisted they handle it like victorious soldiers. Interestingly, the New Testament writers sensed no quandary over the topic of Satan and demons as we do today. The apostle Paul referred often to satanic opposition. For New Testament believers spiritual warfare wasn't a metaphor; it was reality.

> "Spiritual Warfare is as old as the garden of Eden. Actually, spiritual warfare predates the creation of man. In Isaiah 14:12-15, we are introduced to a cosmic struggle between Lucifer and Jehovah. In the New Testament, Jesus seems to allude to this event when He says, 'I saw Satan fall like lighting from heaven' (Luke 10:18). Throughout the Bible the purposes of God battle the desires of Satan. These are played out on the stage of the human drama. In Revelation 20:10, the outcome of this spiritual battle is revealed when Satan is 'cast into the lake of fire ... and will be tormented day and night forever and ever."[1]

Note these key postresurrection Scriptures relating to Satan and his activity:

Acts 5:3-4
Romans 16:19-20
2 Corinthians 2:5-11
1 Thessalonians 2:18

WEEKLY SESSION ANNOUNCEMENTS

Obviously our Scripture Premise this week is ALL of them thus far. Eek!

And you don't need me to remind you to rehearse the others.

If you haven't been memorizing them before now, get busy. Don't make me stop this car.

Don't forget to pray for an opportunity to share with someone what you're learning.

Last but not least: Please, please tell me that you served someone!

We live in a world of two kingdoms in conflict—the kingdom of God and the kingdom of darkness. We are engaged in a spiritual battle whether we're active participants or not. "It is not a battle between man and Satan but between Satan and God. Though man is often the focus of Satan's attacks, Satan's purposes do not have to do with the defeat of man but the desire to supplant God."[2]

Satan cannot attack us without permission. We either open the door by giving him a foothold in our lives, or the Lord has allowed it for a time or season. Satan has power, but it's limited in nature. He can only use it within the boundaries God sets for him.

May I also point out what's always at stake? Glory. To whom will we ascribe glory? That is the question.

How can you see God's authority over Satan in Job 1:6-12?

How might this element of Job's story encourage you the next time you face spiritual attack?

Satan's ability to wreak havoc in Job's life came by God's permission and not without reason. God depicted Job as a man of authentic worship. Satan begged to differ. He believed Job's worship depended on God's blessings. In the end, suffering purified Job's worship (42:3-6) and showed Satan wrong. Job did fear God in all things, even through suffering and pain. Oh, that we would be found the same kind of worshipers as Job.

RECOMMENDED READING

Spiritual Warfare
TIMOTHY M. WARNER

The Invisible War
CHIP INGRIM

The Truth About Spiritual Warfare
C. MARK CORTS

If the Lord never did another thing for us, what He has already done more than merits our undying loyalty. Take a few moments to praise "the God and Father of our Lord Jesus Christ, who has blessed us in Christ with every spiritual blessing in the heavens" (Eph. 1:3). **Take time to read over all of your Confidence Boosters and Scripture Premises now.**

Requirement 2
Know the Role Your Identity Plays

In my Sunday morning Bible study we've been studying the Gospel of Luke. In Luke you encounter the topic of spiritual warfare repeatedly. Never in my years of teaching have I seen such a response. Women have lined up telling stories of satanic attacks including onslaughts of nightmares, bouts of bizarre temptations with suicide, sudden dealings with phobic fears, and feeling forgotten and unloved by God. If the stories aren't personal accounts, they relate to someone they know.

According to Ephesians 6 we have the authority to stand against Satan and his tactics. If you're feeling the battle heating up more than ever before, you aren't crazy. The Devil is furious that his time is short (Rev. 12:12). If you're getting more serious about following Jesus Christ, then Satan is more serious about watching your every move. But you want to hear something refreshing? We don't have to be afraid. Keep beholding Jesus.

In connecting all our sessions together, we need to understand that our victory in Christ has everything to do with identifying ourselves with the victorious One. We don't win through our sinlessness. Our victory comes in identifying ourselves with Him in His victorious conquest.

Take a few moments to read through Ephesians 1:3-23, noting how many times Paul used the words "in Him."

From the beginning of week 1, we've poured a heavy foundation of the rich identity we have in Christ. Every Confidence Booster and Scripture Premise exclaims these riches.

We are a **chosen** people.

We are a **redeemed** people.

We are a **promised** people.

We are a **supplied** people.

We are a **commanded** people.

We are a **victorious** people.

Beside each Confidence Booster above, jot some key words from its Scripture Premise.

———————————————

Our job is to prayerfully live from our new identities by standing secure in Christ. When we do, we seize victorious living. This is why we need to memorize our Confidence Boosters and Scripture Premises. When the enemy attacks us—and he will—we have a base of truth to stand on against him. Remember when I said in the introduction that I wanted to bring you to a place where you put your foot down and say, "Enough is enough"? Well, here's the spot. It's time to claim your identity in Christ and stand against the enemy.

For whatever reason, God has thrown me into this topic of spiritual warfare. I surely wasn't looking to learn. Before I even became a Christian, I attended a gathering on prayer where they talked about spiritual warfare. I had never even heard the term; but being hungry for God, I took lots of notes.

I ended up getting saved that day. Maybe it scared me to a decision. Because Halloween was just a few days away, someone handed me two books—one on Halloween and one about Satan. I was an avid reader and deeply desirous for spiritual things, so I ignorantly and quickly dove in. It wasn't long before I was scared to death. Fortunately, not only did it scare me but it also forced me to God's Word.

Within a few short years I encountered a demonized relative. Family members considered me a strong Christian and wanted my help. I sought counsel from my church and took this relative in for prayer. Sadly, the person left as bound as they came, and the situation got far worse.

The level of attacks I experienced afterward was, at times, unbearable. Through my relative, Satan vehemently reminded me of the person I was before I met Christ. He tried to use my Christianity against me.

My heart was broken over my loved one's captivity. I wanted this person free. I've said many, many times in face-to-face conversations, "Jesus will set you free. He will love you, forgive you, and take all that torment away. You do not have to live in this darkness. You can be free. Turn to Jesus. Please turn to Jesus." To this day my loved one has not, and it pains me greatly. I'm convinced the problem is not Jesus' inability but only a lack of this person's repentance.

God powerfully used this relative to open my eyes to the reality of spiritual warfare. I was so young in my faith that I had no idea how uncommon it was for a churched person to see or encounter such a thing. The experience also exponentially ushered in my healing and restoration. I saw who was behind all my heartache and pain. I observed the astounding authority of God. When the ministers commanded those demons to be quiet in Jesus' name, they listened. All the demons in hell are no match for God.

All of a sudden, when I read Luke 10:1-20, it made perfect sense. In the passage we behold Satan's kingdom defeated—through Jesus' disciples. Please read Luke 10:1-20.

When Jesus sent His disciples out to minister, what did He give them (v. 19)?

Why were the disciples so joyful when they returned (v. 17)?

What did Jesus offer them in the middle of their rejoicing (v. 20)?

When we obey the Lord and it works, isn't the feeling amazing? Not only were the disciples getting a kick out of the situation but so was Jesus. In one breath Jesus said, "Keep your perspective, boys. Rejoice in the right thing, in your salvation." But in the next breath, with ecstatic joy He basically exclaimed to His Father: "Yea! They're getting it!" You can see what I mean in the rest of the story in Luke 10:21-24.

The disciples weren't the only ones Jesus wanted to get it.

What was Adam's job in the garden of Eden (Gen. 2:15)?

Would you believe the words to "watch over" come from a Hebrew word that means "to guard, to be careful, to watch carefully over and to be on one's guard"?[3] Obviously Adam didn't do a very good job watching over the garden, did he?

The enemy is still ever on the prowl. How are we guarding the garden of our lives? Christ has afforded us a holy do-over in guarding our gardens.

How does this principle of guarding our lives connect with week 4 and our need for regular repentance, crop inspections, and daily consecration?

What can you trust God to do in your stand against Satan (2 Thess. 3:3)?

Requirement 3

Recognize and Resist Satan's Attacks

Recently I hosted an impromptu Q&A with my extended family about the satanic attacks they personally experience. Over Thanksgiving dinner no less—don't you wish you were in my family? Now I wouldn't suggest you try this on unbelieving relatives or you're likely to clear the room.

Whether or not they thought it was a sweet moment, I did. I so loved hearing their responses. I'll give you a synopsis.

Question 1—How do you know when the Devil is attacking you?

They cited feelings of worthlessness, hopelessness, overwhelming fear, discouragement, insecurity, and temptation. They feel misunderstood, easily angered, experience lots of self doubt, feel extreme humiliation, and shame. Some struggle with depression, restlessness, anxiousness, and insomnia. They sometimes question the reality of their faith, question the love and care of God, have no peace, and feel beaten down and consumed with self.

Question 2—What do you do when you're feeling attacked?

They busy themselves. Crawl into a hole and isolate. Put worship music on in their ears. Get out and serve somebody so as to get their focus off themselves. Turn their anger inward. Go shopping. Reach for alternative sources of comfort, which have been at times alcohol and food. Overcompensate by controlling their environments. Finally, hope it ends soon.

1. **How do you know when the Devil attacks you?**
   ○ **feel overwhelmed with fear** ○ **feel worthless and ashamed**
   ○ **question God and His love** ○ **am easily angered and agitated**

2. **What do you do when you're feeling attacked?**
   ○ **isolate** ○ **busy myself**
   ○ **get down on myself** ○ **cry out to the Lord**

3. **Has the enemy been trying to keep you from sharing and serving?**
   ○ **Yes—I've hardly shared or served.**
   ○ **Yes—but I've been pushing through the resistance.**
   ○ **Yes—but I've really enjoyed it.**
   ○ _____ .

Consider starting a conversation with a friend using these same questions.

Feeling a strong sense of oppression is one way I know the enemy is attacking me. It's like depression but different. Someone once said it's like trying to operate in mud. I see this repeatedly in teaching my Sunday morning class. I can be prayed up, ready for the lesson, happy in Jesus, walk into the room, and wham. Suddenly I cannot sense the Lord's presence. I feel spiritually confused, down in spirit, and want to go home.

Thankfully, I've learned that it's not about me. In the beginning, I'd take it personally and think something was wrong with me. Now I recognize it as warfare. Usually when I begin reading the Scriptures, it lifts. But if not, I press through by standing firm in the Lord and continue on.

When the Devil attacks, it usually encompasses an onslaught of arresting emotions and thoughts. Besides the feeling of oppression, the Devil likes to hit me with self-hate and self-rejection.

A little sister in the faith recently called to tell me that she needed to talk. When I heard a quiver in her voice, I insisted she open up and tell me immediately. In tears she began explaining that for the last several weeks she had been enduring episodes of intense loneliness, fear, and discouragement. These feelings came coupled with episodes of hearing a frightening gunshot sounds that came with the suggestion: "You know, this could all be over in an instant. No more pain." Then an eerie stillness would settle on her as if the situation had actually played out.

As you can imagine, I was highly concerned and went into full-blown teaching mode. I'm sure I explained and over explained what I will condense here for you. You better know I was ticked at the Devil. This young woman is godly, and I've been watching God raise her up in a mighty way. She's got the gift of teaching and even more than that, the heart of a student. She is passionate about God's Word, and I can assure you, the Devil is alarmed.

The first thing I asked was, "Kim, how are you resisting the Devil?" When she responded, "Well, I've been praying, quoting Scripture, and trying to praise Jesus," I began to teach her this …

In James 4:7 in the margin, circle the two components necessary for the enemy to flee.

> "Submit yourselves, then, to God. Resist the devil, and he will flee from you."
> **JAMES 4:7, NIV**

Many have the submitting part down. They pray. They praise. They worship. But they do not stand firm and resist the enemy. We do not have to give in to Satan's attacks, barely getting by. **Our God dwells within us, and mighty is His name.** We can stand and resist the Devil.

Guess what? My friend took Scripture's advice, and it worked. Sister, it's Ephesians 6:10-18 coming to life. **Please reread that passage now, taking notice of the words "stand" and "resist" (v. 13).**

Against whom do we fight a battle necessitating armor (vv. 11-12)?

The Greek word for *"tactics"* (some translations use "schemes") is *methodeia*. It's where we get our English word *method*. In the fullest sense the term means, "to work by method … the following or pursuing of an orderly and technical procedure."[4] In laymen's terms Satan studies us to see how and where he can best get to us. He does his homework.

In what ways do these verses encourage us not to be afraid?

2 Chronicles 20:17

1 Corinthians 15:57-58

Standing firm in the Lord means being utterly convinced of what God says as our final authority. It means we live abandoned to and wholly unified with the Spirit of God within us, trusting fully in His protection and strength.

How do you see this at work in Paul's letter to Timothy (2 Tim. 4:16-18)?

We must recognize that **we do not fight *for* victory, we fight *from* victory.** Which means, "When we fight, we're not trying to win. We're just enforcing the victory Jesus has already secured."[5]

How does this concept—fighting *from* a place of victory rather than fighting *for* a place of victory—change your idea of warfare?

Which would you say you lean more toward? Explain.
○ fighting for victory   ○ fighting from victory

Sometime this week take a few minutes to ponder the power of your victorious God expressed in Colossians 1:13-20 and 2:9-15. Ask the Lord, the Ruler of all, to come and live His life through you in much greater victory than you've ever known before.

Stand Firm in the Armor of God

We will consider the armor of God in three segments.
First we'll look at truth, righteousness, and peace. Then we'll consider faith, salvation, and with a sword. Finally we'll examine Spirit-led prayer.

In Truth, Righteousness, and Peace

My dear friend, Shannon, told me the coolest story about her middle child. He had asked if he could hold his baby sister, and Shannon nonchalantly replied, "Of course you can hold her, Jack. You're her big brother." Looking rather puzzled he replied, "I am?" "Well, of course you are."

Suddenly her little dude took on a brand-new persona. His shoulders popped up, his chest poked out, and a confident new swagger appeared in his step. She was certain he'd never thought of himself in such strong terms. Perhaps Emma's *little* brother. But never Olivia's *big* brother.

Victorious. Do we really see ourselves in such strong terms? It's possible our spiritual shoulders might pop up, our spiritual chests might stick out, and a confident new swagger might appear in our step. After all, we *are* the children of the Most High God, and He has rescued us from the dominion of darkness and brought us into the kingdom of the Son He loves (Col. 1:15).

I'm not talking about spiritual pride. I'm talking about believing, really believing, that we are the chosen, redeemed, promised, supplied, commanded, and victorious people of God.

> **Imagine what would happen if the church worldwide thought of herself in such strong terms. How might we act differently if we did?**
>
> **Are you beginning to think of yourself in such strong terms? If so, how?**
>
> **Reread Ephesians 6:10-18, and write verse 10 below.**

My commentaries agree that Paul's admonition to "be strong in the Lord" (NIV) means that we are to allow Him to strengthen us as we strengthen ourselves in the Lord. "To be strong in the Lord" by "putting on the full armor of God" establishes in the life of the believer what Dr. Constable describes as "divine enabling" and "human co-operation."[6] So, in divine enabling and human cooperation let's get active in our armor.

What is the first piece of armor (v. 14)?

Scholars widely believe Paul was sizing up the Roman soldier who was guarding him in prison when he penned this particular metaphor (Acts 28:16).

Look closely at the word "truth" in the first piece of the armor. This means the whole gospel truth works itself out in our lives as "purity from all error or falsehood" and "in true and sincere holiness."[7] It means righteousness in action. We don't just speak truth; we live truth.

> "Surely You desire integrity in the inner self, and You teach me wisdom deep within."
>
> **PSALM 51:6**

> "You supported me because of my integrity and set me in Your presence forever."
>
> **PSALM 41:12**

With this in mind, compare Psalm 51:6 and Psalm 41:12 in the margin.

Why do you think integrity is so important? What does Ephesians 6:12 suggest about integrity?

When we stand firm with truth like a belt around our waist, we overcome Satan through a lifestyle that conforms to the Lord's commands. We exhibit a consistency of truth on our lips and in our lives. We cannot truly resist Satan if our walk doesn't match our talk. The enemy fights with deception. We must fight with divine power and human cooperation.

What is the second piece of armor?

_____ like armor on your _____ (v. 14)

The breastplate covered the soldier's body from his neck to his thighs with the critical duty of protecting his heart. Some say if the sun was shining the light reflecting from the breastplates of Roman soldiers could blind the enemy.

According to Ephesians 5:8, what are you in the Lord?

Can you imagine that standing firm in the righteousness of Christ shines a radiant light in the spirit world? It has the power to blind your enemy. What if the next time the enemy came at you, you practiced your second Confidence Booster: In Christ, you are redeemed. Christ has clothed you, cleansed you, and communes with you. After all, the third piece of armor promises a sure footing.

What is the third piece of armor?

The readiness that comes from the gospel of _____ **(v. 15)**

A Roman soldier wore sandals thickly studded with nails for traction. Only through the truth of the gospel can we stand firm against temptation when we are attacked. Note in what we stand firm—peace.

Girlfriend, you and I are to be so familiar with the gospel that we can recognize truth from the Devil's deceptions and immediately share it with ourselves. Isaiah 26:3 says God will keep "the mind that is dependent on You in perfect peace, for it is trusting in you."

What state of mind does trusting God bring?

In what ways has Satan been working to steal your peace?

_____

○ **your work—too much pressure**
○ **your church—disunity and division**
○ **your heart—consumed with worry**
○ **your relationships—strife and uncertainty**

The Roman soldiers soles were thickly studded with nails for traction. We can stand secure by the nails of our Savior. He is our trust, our hope, and our stay. Let's put our foot down. Enough is enough. We overcome in Christ's truth, righteousness, and peace. Now let's consider the next three parts of God's armor for us.

In Faith, Salvation, and with a Sword

I confess I haven't always known what the armor of God really means. Teaching a Sunday morning Bible study forced me to study the armor in-depth, and I was blown away. What I realized was it had everything to do with my identification with Jesus and living a lifestyle of faith. I found that standing strong against Satan's schemes happens when we live a daily lifestyle of abandonment to Jesus Christ. Within this portion we will wrap up the last three pieces of our armor.

What is the fourth piece of armor?
The shield of _____ **(v. 16)**

The shield was a large, oblong piece the Roman soldier used as a protective weapon that consisted of "two layers of wood glued together, covered with linen and hide, and bound with iron. Soldiers often fought side by side with a solid wall of shields. But even a single-handed combatant found himself sufficiently protected."[8] Interestingly, this is the only occasion Paul indicated the *effect* of a particular piece of armor.

What happens to the flaming arrow of the enemy
when you hold up your shield of faith (v. 16)?

The shield of faith completely snuffs out the fire of the enemy. When we firmly resolve to believe the truth of God's Word and hold it high as our protection, it doesn't just deflect Satan's flaming arrow, it completely extinguishes his fire.

"Herodotus described how cane darts tipped with tow were dipped in pitch and then ignited."[9] The enemy does exactly the same thing, only his pitch is a concoction of condemnation, accusation, persecution, hopelessness, fear, discouragement, false teaching, despair, and criticism. When Satan is finished with you, you're not just singed in your faith. He wants to leave you feeling absolutely scorched. Satan can never destroy a believer, but he can sure make us feel like we've been destroyed (2 Cor. 4:7-12). We must not be fooled. Satan is aiming to burn us in every sense of the word.

Sadly, we hardly ever burn alone. Have you noticed how quickly fire spreads? Satan wants to utterly burn our families, our marriages, our friendships, and our reputations.

Girlfriend, when we play with the Devil, we are looking to get burned. Flirting with temptation never equals satisfaction and acceptance in the end. Only "suppering" with Jesus, eating of the rich bread of His presence and drinking deep of His cleansing blood, will ultimately bring deep comfort and satisfaction.

God wants to teach us to stand firm and raise our shields of faith.

Is someone you know flirting with Satan's temptation or under his assault? If so, write his or her initials here _____ and pray for the person now.

What is the fifth piece of armor? The helmet of _____ (v. 17)?

Our minds are our most sensitive area. All our living funnels through our minds first.

Commentaries agree that the helmet of salvation hinges on a present-salvation experience versus a past-salvation experience. Paul focused on the Lord being our present deliverance. Constable says: "Confidence in God becomes our salvation and so protects our thinking when we are under attack."[10]

When the enemy attacks, we first lose perspective in our minds. Thus we need our helmet of salvation constantly. Our minds don't have to run hysterically into high gear with "What if?" and "Oh, no," and "I don't know what I'm going to do." You and I can deflect from fear, constant second-guessing, and the ever-pressing need to know what will happen next because Jesus has saved us, Jesus is saving us, and Jesus will continue to save us.

Describe a time when the enemy made a "mountain out of a molehill" in your life. How did the Lord give you clarity through His present salvation?

Do you need to trust the Lord again to do this for you now? If so, confess it to Him.

_____

What is the sixth piece of armor?
The _____ of the Spirit (v. 17)

Scholars say a Roman soldier's sword wasn't long but rather light as to be used in hand-to-hand combat. Soldiers spent many hours honing their skills. Knowing their sword was like knowing their hand. Truly having a tight grip on it was a matter of life and death.

Surprisingly, the sword of the Spirit is the only piece of equipment that tells us verbatim what it *is*. The shield of faith explains what it *does*, but not necessarily what it *is*.

So, what is the sword of the Spirit?

Hebrews 4:12 tells us the Word of God "is living and effective and sharper than any double-edged sword, penetrating as far as the separation of soul and spirit, joints and marrow. It is able to judge the ideas and thoughts of the heart." I can testify that nothing has changed my life more than the Holy Scriptures. I would not be who I am today without them. Sure I'd be saved, but undoubtedly an emotional mess. I am a living, breathing miracle because of God's Word in my life. No drug's high is like encountering the Most High leaping from the pages of the Bible. Believe me, I know. It is where hope is found and lives are restored.

How has God met you and changed you on the pages of His Holy Word?

Behind the concept "word" exist two Greek terms: *logos* and *rhema*.

I love the distinction that *logos* describes the entire Word of God and *rhema* speaks of the applied Word of God. We experience the *rhema* Word for our specific situations. For instance, when Jesus encountered Satan in the wilderness and was tempted, Jesus took the *logos* and turned it into *rhema* when He repeatedly said: "For it is written." Resisting Satan requires us to do the same. Just as a soldier would have a tight grip his sword, we must be women who have a tight grip on ours.

Have you've recently used the *rhema* of God's Word when you didn't know that's what you were doing? When, and what were the circumstances?

Sister, I charge you today to consume larger doses of the logos. Just when you need it most the Holy Spirit then uses the *logos* you store in your heart, applying it as *rhema*. Maybe it's time to try one of those Bible reading plans that's is in the back of your Bible. If yours doesn't have one, try *www.bhpublishinggroup.com/readthebible/reading.asp* for a plan you can use. So when the enemy comes, and he will come, we have the Word to stand against him.

In Spirit-Led Prayer

I am so proud of you for finishing your Bible study I could cry. In fact, tears are welling in my eyes even now. My heart

Confidence Booster and Scripture Premise

Close this portion by repeating your Confidence Boosters and their Scripture Premises. Of course, you may write them out too.

Reflect on your favorite memory of how God led you to share the truths you've been studying. How did it transpire and what blessed you most?

beats for leading women to feast on God's Word. I've often said, "If women are serious about walking with Jesus, I'm so happy to show them how."

You have been that serious woman. I have loved sharing time in God's Word and, I hope, some encouragement.

Compare your current understanding of God's attitude towards you with your understanding prior to this study. What has been the most significant change you've seen in your relationship with God?

As we complete our Bible study, please read Ephesians 6:10-18.

With what did the apostle Paul conclude verse 18?

Although scholars differ on whether prayer is an actual piece of the armor, we must recognize that we battle within the context of prayer. Some would say when you read the text in the Greek it's as if Paul didn't even take a breath between verses 17 and 18, but prayer absolutely fits whether or not it's part of the actual armor. Any kind of intimacy with our God always begins and ends with prayer. Any kind of realized victory begins and ends with prayer, too.

One of my favorite resources describes prayer as "an exchange of confidence: we assume the stance of a trusting child and pray with faith that is matched by obedience; God remembers our frailty, loves us as his children, hears and answers our prayers."[11]

Isn't that the best quote you've heard on prayer?

Turn to Hebrews 4:16, and reread it with an "exchange of confidence" in mind. How is this verse different to you now than when you first began this study?

My sister, wearing your armor means wrapping your life up in Christ's life; it denotes being fully confident in Him. It's submitting yourself to God's truth as your governing rule for obedient living. It's believing in the victorious supply of the Spirit and prayerfully seeking His leadership in every area of your life. As E. M Bounds wrote in *The Necessity of Prayer:*

> "The life of a Christian is a warfare, an intense conflict, a lifelong contest. It is a battle, moreover, waged against invisible foes, who are ever alert, and ever seeking to entrap, deceive, and ruin the souls of men. The life to which Holy Scripture calls men is no picnic, or holiday junketing. It is no pastime, no pleasure jaunt. It entails effort, wrestling, struggling; it demands the putting forth of the full energy of the spirit in order to frustrate the foe and to come off, at the last, more than conqueror. It is no primrose path, no rose-scented dalliance. From start to finish, it is war."[12]

With that said, our six weeks of homework has been no holiday junket, though I have treasured your company. You have fought for your delight in Jesus, and I applaud you. Now you can wake up every morning in the welcoming light of the Lord's presence all around you. Why? Because you have been blessed in Christ with every spiritual blessing in the heavens (Eph. 1:3).

wrapping things up

As God Has Commanded, These Are Your Rights!

1. You have the right to live in the delight of God's choosing of you.

     no more guilt, shame, and condemnation

2. You have the right to live in the delight of God's redemption of you.

     no more spiritual perfectionism, only rich acceptance and satisfaction

3. You have the right to live in the delight of God's promise of His Spirit.

     no more broken promises and self-determination

4. You have the right to live in the delight of God's supply of His Spirit.

     no more powerlessness and sinful harvests

5. You have the right to live in the delight of God's command of love.

     no more dread of having to love God and others

6. You have the right to live in the delight of God's provision of victory.

     no more wishing for the victory Jesus has provided

7. From being chosen to empowered,

     you now have the right to stand up and enjoy your God.

"Now to Him who is able to protect you from stumbling and to m
the presence of His glory, blameless and with great joy, to the on
through Jesus Christ our Lord, be glory, majesty, power, and au
time, now and forever. Amen" (Jude 24-25).

Father, my delight in
You really comes down to
trust, doesn't it? Will I trust that You
have come after me and chosen me to be Yours?
Will I trust that You have redeemed me to feast on
Your rich acceptance and satisfaction? Will I trust that You
have promised me Your Spirit, coming to live Your life in me?
Will I trust that You are my Rock who holds me together? Will I
trust that You supply me with the power, being all that I cannot? Will
I trust that You transform me from the inside out? Will I trust that You
command me to love—knowing my greatest joy comes when I abide
in Your love, even toward others? Will I trust that You have won the
battle forevermore and I can stand victoriously by Your side?

Now I see and know.

It's when I wholly trust in Your provision,
I escape duty and enter delight.

In Jesus' name keep me resting in these
truths forever. Amen.

....

1. C. Mark Corts, *The Truth About Spiritual Warfare* (Nashville: B&H Publishing Group, 2006), xi.

2. Ibid.

3. Warren Baker, Eugene Carpenter, *The Complete Word Study Dictionary* (Chattanooga, TN: AMG Publishers, 2003).

4. Spiro Zodhiates, gen. ed., *Key Word Study Bible* (Chattanooga, TN: AMG Publishers, 1996), 1650.

5. Chip Ingram, *The Invisible War* (Grand Rapids, MI: Baker Books, 2006), 61.

6. Thomas L. Constable, "Notes on Ephesians" (Sonic Light, 2010), 74.

7. Spiro Zodhiates, *The Complete Word Study Dictionary* (Chattanooga, TN: AMG Publishers, 1992), 120.

8. Frank E. Gaebelein, ed., *Expositor's Bible Commentary* (Grand Rapids, MI: Zondervan, 1982), 88.

9. Ibid.

10. Constable, 77.

11. Leland Ryken, James C. Wilhoit, Tremper Longman III, gen eds., *Dictionary of Biblical Imagery* (Madison, WI: IVP Academic, 1998), 660.

12. E. M. Bounds, *The Necessity of Prayer* [online] n.d. [cited 19 January 2011]. Available from the Internet: *http://www.worldinvisible.com/library/bounds/5bb.10596-necessity%20of%20prayer/5bb.10596.11.htm*

Leader Guide

We all crave relationships. Both Christians and non-Christians desire to belong to a group—a family of friends they can trust with the truth about who they are. As a leader, you have the opportunity to foster something powerful—biblical community. As you spend time with your group, pray with them and serve them in unexpected ways. When you lay that foundation of trust and belonging, you enable God to transform the lives of your group members. No longer is Bible study just an isolated hour of teacher-student interaction; it goes deeper—building lasting community that influences our lives and the very threads of who we are.

If you're wondering, *"What did I sign up for?"* Go to *lifeway.com/tammiehead* for video clips, additional leader helps, and suggested service opportunities. **I highly encourage you to check it out.**

✳ Consider creative ways to motivate members to memorize the Confidence Boosters and Scripture Premises. Rewards (stickers, candies, Post-it® notes, pens) work wonders and create an atmosphere of fun.

✳ Don't forget to share personal stories from week to week of how God is encouraging you to share with others what He is teaching you.

✳ Consider creating a *Duty or Delight* Facebook™ group to foster community.

Introduction

Get acquainted by group members sharing a bit about themselves.

 ✳ Identify at least one quirk or idiosyncrasy about yourself.

 ✳ What excites you most about being a part of this study?

Have someone read aloud Ephesians 1:3-4.

 ✳ How does this passage express the heart of God toward His creation?

 ✳ Why is it so difficult for people to believe God loves them personally?

Pray together, asking God to do a fresh work of delight in members' lives.

Encourage the women to read the Introduction. Discuss service opportunities your group can do. Begin a plan to serve together as part of your group experience.

If you created a Facebook group, inform members. Post on their walls, and send announcements about the coming week. If Facebook isn't an option, consider writing members a note expressing your joy that they are part of the group.

Session One:
Knowing God Has Chosen Us

Each member will need one index card for this session.

"God didn't save us so we would keep Him happy. He saved us for soul-satisfying intimacy" (p. 12).

 ✳ With which pitfall (twisted theology, insecurity, fear, shame) do you most often have to deal?

 ✳ In what ways do you see insecurity and spiritual perfectionism in yourself?

"A faith that originates with us paves the way for a lack of spiritual rest" (p. 15).

✳ Read Philippians 1:6, and discuss why a faith that originates with us is a dangerous faith (p. 15).

✳ In what ways does Satan perpetuate guilt in your life? By the way, please apologize for me if any group member is named Sheila.

"What rest our souls can find in the righteousness of Christ" (p. 18).

✳ How will you practice embracing your "rights" in Christ (p. 35)?

Pray. Have members write on their index cards the prevailing lie "Sheila" whispers in their ears. Trade cards within the group, and commit to pray for one another.

Continue planning your group's service project. Begin finalizing details of when and where it will take place.

Close in prayer, offering members the option to voice a prayer too.

Session Two:
Knowing God Has Redeemed Us

"Two cavernous hungers tug at the human soul—hungers for acceptance and for satisfaction" (p. 36).

✳ Which word of advice spoke to you most this week (Eat More Bread, Drink More Blood, Remember Your Redemption)?

✳ Which do you struggle with most—satisfaction or acceptance?

✳ Discuss your thoughts on the concept of *Guilt* or *Conviction* (p. 53).

"Christ has come, through the bread of His body, to supply our hunger for satisfaction with a feast on the bread of His Presence" (p. 38).

✳ Have someone read aloud Genesis 3:6. Discuss how Eve was looking for satisfaction apart from God.

✳ In what ways does God convict you about looking for satisfaction apart from God?

✳ How has God stirred dissatisfaction in you so you would want Him more (p. 44)?

"Some of us have lived in a perpetual state of weariness because we've allowed what our friends do, what our mothers do—perhaps, even what our teachers, preachers, and mentors do—to define what we do" (p. 45).

✳ How did you finish the statement, "I feel so bad that I don't …?"

✳ How have comparisons stolen your ability to delight in God's approval of you?

✳ Share your answers to the question on page 51: "How would you be different tomorrow …"

"Redemption means the sinless Lamb of God was sacrificed on our behalf. We become acceptable to God forevermore. We never have to hide again … We can rest in the Lord's amazing grace" (p. 56).

✳ In what ways will you practice resting in your redemption more?

Close in prayer, thanking God for His crazy love for every group member.

Session Three:
Knowing God Has Promised Us

You'll need one small rock for each member and a few Sharpies.®

"God knows we're a mess. He knows we cannot and will not do this relationship thing unless He comes and does it in us" (p. 64).

✳ How has God's faithfulness of love to His people encouraged you about His love for you in spite of your own struggles with sin?

"Christ coming to live in our hearts is not cute church jargon" (p. 66).

✳ Have someone read the "I will's" of God from Jeremiah 32:40-41.

✳ How do God's "I will's" encourage us to defer to God's supply within us—instead of us trying to walk with God out of sheer determination?

"Could the invisible barriers you have felt with the Lord be walls that you have built" (p. 74)?

✱ In what ways has a divided heart stolen your delight in the Lord?

✱ On what aspect of God's character do you solidly need to stand?

Have members write the aspect of God's character on their rock. Suggest that each of you carry the rock as an act of faith in trusting God more this week. End in prayer.

Session Four:
Knowing God Has Supplied Us

Be prepared for tender emotions this week. Sessions 4 and 5 are the most difficult lessons, so encourage your group to press through to delight.

"How do we trigger more of the Holy Spirit's power in our lives" (p. 84)?

✱ In what areas were you most convicted this week?

"We never have to worry where we stand with God" (p. 88).

✱ Have someone read the Scripture Premise for this week.

✱ How does this verse put all of the weight on God and His provisions for us?

✱ Is God convicting you that transformation is His job? You don't have to prove anything; all you have to do is yield to His Spirit working inside of you.

"What would your life be like if you fully rested in the fact that God has nothing but good for you" (p. 88)?

✱ How has/is God using *People, Pressures,* and *Problems* to prune you?

✱ In what ways have you held back from all-out surrender? How has this had a direct affect in how much you've enjoyed the Lord?

Consider praying over those in especially difficult situations this session.

Session Five:
Knowing God Has Commanded Us to Love

"One of the greatest paradoxes of the human soul is love" (p. 108).

* ✻ How does this week's lesson bring together all the previous lessons?
* ✻ How did the Confidence Booster "I Can Do This Thing!" hit you this week in regard to being truly able to love God and people because His Spirit is your supply?
* ✻ Discuss how our choice to disobey the Great Commandment directly affects our delight in God.

"Many do not advance in Christian progress because they stick in penances and particular exercises while neglecting the love of God, which must be the end purpose of all actions" (p. 111).

* ✻ What were your thoughts on Tammie's counselor insisting she lay down her quiet time (p. 112)?
* ✻ How did you answer the question on page 113?

"Beloved, we quench the Spirit quickly when we mistreat and dishonor people" (p. 120).

* ✻ How does consistent *Jesus Time* directly affect your delight in the Lord?
* ✻ In what ways were you convicted with how you treat people?

Close in prayer, asking God to do a profound work of healing in relationships.

Session Six:
Knowing God Has Secured Our Victory

Consider having a celebration this week. Hosting a potluck can be loads of fun!

"In connecting all of our sessions together, we need to understand that our victory in Christ has everything to do with our identifying ourselves with the victorious One" (p. 134).

* ❋ How did the Confidence Boosters and Scripture Premises come together for you this week?
* ❋ In what ways does not understanding your identity in Christ directly affect your ability to delight in your relationship with God?
* ❋ How do you see the armor of God differently?

"Standing firm in the Lord means being utterly convinced of what God says as our final authority" (p. 140).

* ❋ Have someone read aloud James 4:7.
* ❋ How did you answer the three questions on page 138?
* ❋ Discuss the two components needed for the enemy to flee and how this spoke to you personally.

"We must recognize that 'we do not fight for victory, we fight from victory,' which means, 'When we fight, we're not trying to win. We're just enforcing the victory Jesus has already secured'" (p. 140).

* ❋ In what ways did this concept change your idea of daily victory?

"My sister, wearing your armor means wrapping your life up in Christ's life; it denotes being fully confident in Him. It's submitting yourself to God's truth as your governing rule for obedient living. It's believing in the victorious supply of the Spirit, and prayerfully seeking His leadership in every area of your life" (p. 149).

* ❋ How does this statement proclaim a "holy do-over" for us from what happened in the garden with Adam and Eve?
* ❋ Share your answer from page 148, "*Compared to when ...*"
* ❋ How does knowing you're "chosen" exchange a duty mentality for delight?

Close in prayer by thanking God for all that He's done and will continue to do in each of your lives.

BECAUSE
ONE EVENT
CAN CHANGE
YOUR LIFE

LIFEWAY WOMEN EVENTS

lifeway.com/women | 800.254.2022

LifeWay | **Women**